SO-BJN-288

# SONGS

FROM THE

## RESTORATION THEATER

Da Capo Press Music Reprint Series

GENERAL EDITOR

FREDERICK FREEDMAN

VASSAR COLLEGE

WILLARD THORP

# SONGS

## FROM THE

# RESTORATION THEATER

𝄞 DA CAPO PRESS · NEW YORK · 1970

A Da Capo Press Reprint Edition

This Da Capo Press edition of *Songs from the Restoration Theater* is an unabridged republication of the first edition published in Princeton, New Jersey, in 1934. It is published by special arrangement with Princeton University Press.

*Library of Congress Catalog Card Number 76-102003*

SBN 306-71867-7

A Division of Plenum Publishing Corporation
227 West 17th Street
New York, N.Y. 10011

Manufactured in the United States of America

# SONGS FROM THE
# RESTORATION THEATER

*LONDON: HUMPHREY MILFORD*
*OXFORD UNIVERSITY PRESS*

# SONGS

## FROM THE

# RESTORATION THEATER

EDITED BY

## WILLARD THORP

ASSISTANT PROFESSOR OF ENGLISH IN PRINCETON UNIVERSITY

1934

*PRINCETON*

PRINCETON UNIVERSITY PRESS

PRINTED AT THE PRINCETON UNIVERSITY PRESS
PRINCETON, NEW JERSEY, U. S. A.

*For*
*M. F. T.*

# TABLE OF CONTENTS

# INTRODUCTION

But how & by what stepps musick shot up into such request, as to crowd out from ye stage even comedy itself, and to sit downe in her place & become of such mighty value & price as wee now know it to be, is worth Inquiring after.

North, *Musicall Gramarian.*

The intellectual and aesthetic affinities between periods are often easier to discern than to explain. Yet it is not difficult to see why the age of the Restoration, once Macaulay's interdiction had been removed by the modern revulsion from the morality of his class, should find in our time its apologists and admirers. An age which has Dryden for its critic, Purcell for its composer, Wren for its builder and Newton for its scientist, after prejudice vanishes, is not particularly in need of defense. Still even those who have at last discovered its greatness are inadvertently inclined to deprecate its universal measure of witty and delightful living as the idea of the good life. We perhaps still envy in secret Rochester and Sedley as the Puritans envied the spectators at the bear garden.

The songs from the Restoration theater which this book contains were a part of the era's apparatus of pleasure which is still suspect. They are trivial, though of an exquisite triviality, and their significant popularity is the chief warrant for their resurrection in a solemn book published by a university press. For without a knowledge of them even the historian of the drama will read his plays as if they were *libretti.* The members of the audience did not crowd merely to listen to plays; they came to be assaulted on all the senses by the *ensemble* of scenes, machines, dancing and music. They did not object to an occasional infusion of pure drama, a luxurious benevolence of which the playwrights complain incessantly:

> *Now you come hither but to make your Court:*
> *Or from adjacent Coffee Houses throng*
> *At our fourth Act for a new Dance or Song.*
> Prologue to *Bellamira,* 1687

One surmises, indeed, that it was most often the music which held the ears and closed the mouths of the noisy wits in the boxes. This was true, at least, of many, as the unbiased testimony of the Italian Count Magalotti in 1669 affirms: "Before the comedy begins, that the audience may not be tired with waiting, the most delightful symphonies are played; on which account many persons come early to enjoy this agreeable amusement."[1]

The art of music was as widely practised and understood in this age as in the Elizabethan. Charles set the example. With a wave of the royal hand he banished the antique style of the "fancies" and summoned his four and twenty fiddlers to replace his father's consort of

---

[1] *Travels . . . Through England, During the Reign of King Charles The Second,* London, 1821, p. 191.

viols. It is true he approved only of the soft vein and preferred the "step tripla" because he could keep time to it with head and toe, but he did more for music than any other English sovereign and placed it next after his mistresses and his navy in his affectionate regard. One can scarcely mention a great name of the era without associating with it some anecdote of musical history. Pepys's performance on the flageolet, the lute, the fiddle, the viols, the recorder and even the humble parallelogram frequently carried him off into an ecstasy of delight. Evelyn had been trained in the art. L'Estrange's performance on the bass viol could be endured. The elder North, Charles, was able to "play his part exceeding well at first sight" and Francis, his son, the distinguished Lord Keeper, included music among the polite studies which had made life worth living. Hortensia, Duchess of Mazarin, in exile in London, engaged the principal female performers from the theaters to delight the Duke of Buckingham and St.-Evremond who fought out the burning issue of the hour, the propriety of the introduction of opera into England, in her drawing room in Chelsea. And the Anglicized Frenchman himself, though he ridiculed the conventions of the opera, is convicted of having written an "Idyle," composed the music for it and persuaded Madame Mazarin to sing a part in it. On one occasion when the Duke of Buckingham's cabinet was broken open, in a search for treasonous matter, nothing was to be found save some "tunes prickt on severall papers with the Duke's owne hand."

The era witnessed the establishment of public concerts in England and the emergence of the professional musician whose livelihood did not depend on his position in a great house or an ecclesiastical foundation. Several new institutions, developed during these years, indicate a revolutionary change in the function and status of music in the new society. The performers and composers achieved, for example, a kind of monopolistic trade union of their own, "The Corporacion for Regulating the Art and Science of Musique," which during the 1660's could display on its minute book such powerful names as Nicholas Lanier, Banister, Humphrey, Marsh, Blow, Staggins and Turner. In 1683 the first of the St. Cecilia's Day celebrations inaugurated the series of yearly festivals in honor of the patron saint. In the course of twenty years some of the finest music of the age was composed to her glory by King, Draghi, Eccles, Purcell and Clarke with the poetical assistance of librettists like Tate, Shadwell, Dryden, D'Urfey and Congreve. The gentry of various shires resident in London required music for their annual feast days, a custom which spread gradually into the provinces. These affairs increased in splendor until when Purcell's great Yorkshire Feast Song, to words by D'Urfey, was performed in 1690 the costs of presentation mounted to £100.

Beginning in 1672 with the project of "old Banister," whose loss of favor at Court forced him to invent ways of supplementing his income, the institution of the public concert flourished apace. Its history has not yet been written, though the various undertakings can easily be followed in the *London Gazette*. They ranged in quality from the ultra-fashionable performances provided by Franck and King in Charles Street, Covent Garden, and other series at York Buildings and at Chelsea College, to the more vulgar entertainments in the Music-House at the Mitre, near Paul's, and Francis Forcer's establishment at Sadler's Wells. In the more exclusive houses the chief *virtuosi* came direct from the theaters, and in all of them, even to the lowest, the latest tunes from the plays were demanded. Ned Ward strolling through Bartholomew Fair on one of his spying expeditions hears "a most admirable new Ballad, Sung in two parts by Seven Voices." He commands the drawer to ask the singers if they are not performing the "cat-catch." They reply, "No . . . a very fine *Play-House Song,* set by the best Composer in *England.* Why then, said I, pray tell your *Songsters,* they deserve to be Whipt at the *Carts-Arse* for attempting to Sing it. . . ."[2]

At the same time the private music meeting, conducted in imitation of these public concerts, became one of the chief diversions of society. The performers were mainly amateurs, though the wealthy always enticed at least one great lion from the theater or the King's establishment to give the evening the required snobbish distinction. The dramatists found abundant material for satire in these meetings, particularly in the pretense to musical culture of the patrons. Southerne in *The Maid's Last Prayer* has preserved the type in Sir Symphony. While his group of amateurs struggles under his baton, he airs his comprehension of the excellencies of the piece they are attacking:

O Gad! there's a flat Note! There's art! how surprizingly the Key changes! O law! there's a double relish! I swear, Sir, you have the sweetest little Finger in *England*! ha! that stroak's new; I tremble every inch of me: Now Ladies look to your Hearts—Softly Gentlemen—remember the Eccho [the antiphonal response]—Captain, you play the wrong Tune—O law! my Teeth! my Teeth! for God's sake, Captain, mind your Cittern.—Now the Fuga, bases! agen, agen! Lord! Mr. *Humdrum,* you come in three barrs too soon, Come, now the Song—(Act IV, Scene 2).

One can readily see what the result of this extraordinary preoccupation with music by the fashionable world must have been on the nature of the popular drama and the organization of the theatrical establishment itself. It has become the conventional comment to make on the "decline" of Restoration comedy that the sentimental mode, and what is associated with the new temper—a growing remorse on the part of the dramatists for their shameless past—finally drove wit from the stage. The quotation at the head of this essay and other statements like it which can be adduced, show that at the time the cause was ascribed equally to the phenomenal "shooting up into request" of music.

The extent and the vigor of this incursion of music into the drama can be reckoned in a half dozen significant ways, one of the most striking being the growth and development of the theater orchestra. Tom Killigrew bragged to Pepys on February 12, 1667, that "heretofore" the band consisted of only two or three fiddlers but now, owing to his exertions, there are "nine or ten of the best." The French visitor Chappuzeau is amazed to find, about the same time, that in the English theaters "la Musique y'est excellente & les Ballets magnifiques; Qu'elles n'ont pas moins de douze violons chacune pour les Preludes & pour les Entr-actes."[3] These twelve fiddlers, already twice the number customary in the French theater, were increased to twenty-four for Shadwell's *Tempest* (1674). As the musical requirements of the dramatists grew, the orchestra continued to be expanded for special occasions until for Betterton and Purcell's *Dioclesian,* given in 1690, as well as other dramatic operas of the decade, the strings, flutes, hautboys, trumpets and drums called for in the scoring swelled the number of musicians to about fifty.

To accommodate this enlarged orchestra the old music room, concealed in a loft behind the proscenium and over the scenes, was for these events abandoned and the modern location in the pit assumed. The printed stage directions for Shadwell's *Tempest* specifically note the change: "The Front of the Stage is open'd, and the Band of 24 Violins, with the Harpsicals and Theorbo's which accompany the Voices, are plac'd between the Pit and the Stage. While the Overture is playing, the Curtain rises, and discovers a new Frontispiece, joined to the great Pilasters, on each side of the Stage." The experiment had already been tried in the new Theatre Royal in 1663, for Pepys complains that "the musique being below, and most of it sounding under the very stage, there is no hearing of the bases at all, nor very well of the trebles, which sure must be mended" [May 8, 1663]. Although it is possible to cite instances of the orchestra's performing in the new location, Mr. Lawrence is certainly right in his belief that not until the 1690's was it settled there during the whole of an ordinary production.[4] The change is, however, more significant than at first it might seem. The old attitude regarded the instrumental music as an invisible supplement to the action at appropriate places, and the musicians themselves actually preferred to be out of the sight of the audience. The new arrangement treated them as the equals of the players and their performance as equally entertaining to watch.

During the whole period under consideration the chief actors were required, as a part of their regular duties, to perform as singers. A multitude of names leaps to the pen at once: Knipp whom Pepys loved first for the divine way she sang his songs and later for more intimate favors; Moll Davis whose pitiful song in *The Rivals* raised her to a Bed Royal; Mrs. Bracegirdle and Mrs. Butler; Bowman and Betterton and Wilks; Mountfort and Mohun; and for mock-songs in comic rôles, Doggett and Leigh and Haynes. Their duties included singing between the acts and in the musical interludes for which polite taste hankered. By 1690, however, the fastidious public was not entirely satisfied with their pedestrian talents and the theater was obliged to secure *virtuosi* singers like young Jemmy Bowen, Miss Cross, Mrs.

[3] *L'Europe Vivante,* 1667, p. 215.
[4] W. J. Lawrence, "The English Theatre Orchestra," *Musical Quarterly,* 1917, p. 25.

Ayliff and Mrs. Hudson who could execute more justly the roulades and ornaments prescribed by Purcell and Courteville. "Many persons come," North[5] objects, "to hear that single voice, who care not for all the rest, especially If it be a fair Lady; And observing ye discours of the Quallity crittiques, I found it runs most upon ye point, who sings best? and not whither ye musick be good, and wherein?" The chronological arrangement of the songs in this volume shows by a casual turning of the leaves the sudden increase in difficulty of the theatrical music at the end of the era which was responsible for, or was at least concurrent with, this new professionalism.

Historians of the drama have noted the dominant vogue in the last decade of the century of the musical play, a type which can only be defined somewhat loosely as a drama that exists mainly for the songs worked into the scenes. It is distinguished from the *bona fide* play which contains a large number of quite incidental songs and from the semi-opera which aims at establishing an heroic mood by the assistance of particular kinds of musical accompaniment. An outstanding example is *The Comical History of Don Quixote* (1694-1695), D'Urfey's three-part venture, which succeeded admirably in the first two instalments but failed in the third because of hurried preparation and a fatal first performance. Motteux's *Island Princess*, although it was frequently referred to in the period as an opera, fairly well exemplifies the type. But by far the most striking proof of the gradual usurpation of the drama by the "musical part" emerges from a study of the prevalence of the songs interjected in the ordinary comedies and tragedies. During the early days it is unusual to find more than one or two called for, and these are frequently not printed in the text. By the end of the period the usual number has increased to half a dozen, the words are given in full and the music is often appended, with a note on the composers and singers. Dryden's *Indian Emperour* (1667), from which a song is given on p. 14, was interrupted for music only twice; Farquhar's *The Constant Couple* (1699), represented here by the "Damon" song (p. 80), was enlivened in seven places by musical moments.

The compliance of the dramatists with the change was finally won, either through conversion to the new taste or their shrewd recognition of what it would require of them. Shadwell needed no persuasion; he had always been passionately devoted to music and understood more fully the nature of opera than any other playwright in England. His readiness to meet the desires of the public is frankly set forth in the note To the Reader printed in *The Royal Shepherdess* (1669). In taking over the play from Mr. Fountain of Devonshire, he has endeavored to carry on the humors begun by him; "(to satisfie the Concupisence as Mr. *Johnson* calls it, of Jigg and Song) I designed as fit Occasions for them as I could; there being in the former Play but one short Song, which is the last but one."

Dryden seems at first to have been loath to concede a place to music in the theater, as well he might, but after a tentative and dis-

[5] *Musicall Gramarian,* p. 40.

astrous collaboration with Grabu he found a worthy equal in Purcell
on whose account he admitted that music "has since arriv'd to a greater
Perfection in *England*, than ever formerly."

By far the most interesting reflection of the new enthusiasm for the
musical portion of the drama comes from the astounding vogue of
Tom D'Urfey during the last years of the century. As Mr. Day
shows in his *Songs of Thomas D'Urfey* (1933) the solemn spirits despised him humorously as a vulgar hedge-poet, but his songs were on
the lips of everyone. "The trudging Carman whistles your harmonious
Poetry to his Horse, the Glass Coach Beau whispers them to his
senceless Nymph, the Grumbling *Jacobite* mutters them in Corners to
his Abdicated Brethren. . . . Your Ballads, when half asleep, from the
Street, in a high Base and a low Treble, wish me a good rest when
I can catch it. The Cookmaid and Scullion listen to them, and the very
Coachman ingratiates himself to the antiquated Chamber-maid with
them."[6] D'Urfey, who had no serious aims as a dramatist, fills his own
plays with ballads—there are eight songs in *A Fool's Preferment*
(1688)—which were carried hot from the theater by the crowds which
came to hear them as much as to see the play. A year before the failure of Congreve's *The Way of the World* his two-part *Famous History of the Rise and Fall of Massaniello*, helped by Leveridge's popular
fishing song "Of all the world's enjoyments" (p. 78), secured the
favor of the town.

It is natural to wonder why, in view of this steady encroachment
of music on the drama, the opera could not establish itself in England
until the opening of the eighteenth century. There is no call to resurvey
here the history of the English experiments with the form during the
Restoration. Such a summary would have to be largely a condensation
of Professor Dent's *Foundations of English Opera*. But reasons
should be ventured for the tardy acclimatization of the Italian form
and something said of the influence of the prevalent theories of the
opera, for it was constantly a subject for polite conversation, on the
regular drama of the day. One notices, in the first place, that the
English sense of actuality resisted the conventions of the opera
through the entire period. The charge of absurdity is continuously
reiterated from "A Ballad against the Opera" (*Choyce Poems, Being
Songs, Sonnets, Satyrs and Elegies,* 1661) to Dennis's *An Essay on
the Operas after the Italian Manner,* published in 1706. St.-Evre-
mond spoke the sentiments of most downright Englishmen in his letter to the Duke of Buckingham:

There is another thing in *Opera's* so contrary to Nature, that it
always shocks my Imagination, and that is, *the singing the whole from
one End to the other, as if the Persons had ridiculously conspir'd to
treat in Music both of the most common and most important Affairs
of human Life.* Can any Man persuade his Imagination, that a Master
calls his Servant, or sends him of an Errand *singing*? That one Friend
communicates a Secret to another *singing*? That Politicians deliberate

        [6] Quoted by Day, *op. cit.,* p. 31, from *Wit for Money* (1691).

in Council *singing*? That Orders in Time of Battle are given *singing*? And that Men are *melodiously kill'd with Sword, Pike or Musket*?[7]

The desires of the court circle to transplant the French-Italian opera in England issued in little that was constructive. In October of 1660 Charles granted Giulio Gentileschi power to erect an opera house in London and secured him in his monopoly for five years, but none of the vast sums required were promised from the royal purse and the scheme faded into air.[8] Tom Killigrew's plans, enthusiastically outlined to Pepys on August 2, 1664, projected the building of a theater in Moorfields and the bringing over of voices and painters and other persons from Italy to present four operas a year, six weeks at a time. On February 12, 1666/7 at Lord Brouncker's Pepys learned that though these ambitious plans had been abandoned, Killigrew still hoped to present opera at the two public theaters. Actually the first foreign opera to be heard by the public was *Ariane*, presented in French by the recently founded Royal Academy of Music at Drury Lane, March 1673/4. A season of French opera was secured for February of 1685/6. At the court theater in the Great Hall of the royal palace of Whitehall *Rare-en-Tout* was given by a French company on Charles's birthday, May 29, 1677. Cambert, who was in England from 1673 to 1677, possibly produced his *Pomone* during his residence there.

The native writers and composers had meanwhile found the characteristic English compromise in the semi-opera. Even D'Avenant in his earlier experiments departed radically from the Italian and French practice, as Professor Dent observes, by abandoning the required allegorical and classical setting for historical realism, as he understood it. D'Avenant manifestly pointed the way to the English solution in his *Macbeth* (?1663) and *Tempest* (with Dryden, 1667), though it was left to later revivals based on these works to expand to the limit the operatic possibilities of the rites of the weird sisters and the benevolent plots of Ariel. For it was on this feature of the supernatural that the English common sense perversely fixed its approval. Dryden, sensitive always to the precise point at which public taste had arrived, realized this clearly and eventually produced as a result *King Arthur*, with its effective combination of apocryphal British history and supernatural machinery, the finest work in the *genre*.

Before a satisfactory native type was evolved several preliminary experiments had to be made. The *Psyche* (1675) of Locke and Shadwell, adapted from Molière's *comédie-ballet*, attempted to set the fashion in the direction of allegory and myth, but in spite of its great excellence a part of the public objected to it vigorously. Duffet's mock of it, *Psyche Debauch'd*, though a production of the rival house, is by no means to be overlooked in accounting for its failure to reproduce its kind. Dryden had already seen the point when he projected *Albion and Albanius* as a one-act prologue to a longer work which should be

[7] Translation from *The Life of Mr. Thomas Betterton*, 1710, p. 162.
[8] The warrant is published in Miss Eleanore Boswell's *Restoration Court Stage*, 1932, p. 114.

a "Tragedy mix'd with *Opera*; or a *Drama* written in blank Verse, adorn'd with Scenes, Machines, Songs, and Dances: So that the Fable of it is all spoken and acted by the best of the Comedians; the other part of the Entertainment to be perform'd by the same Singers and Dancers, who are introduc'd in this present *Opera*. It cannot properly be called a Play, because the Action of it is supposed to be conducted sometimes by supernatural Means, or Magick; nor an *Opera,* because the Story of it is not sung."[9]

Circumstances obliged him to expand his operatic prologue into a tedious three-act affair which violated in its continuous employment of song and allegory the very principles on which he had announced the longer work was to be built. He was punished by its failure, and we find as a result in *King Arthur*, which was finally written, a perfect balance of the "songish part" with the spoken fable. True to the British contention that only deities and devils and other creatures, such as lovers, madmen and priests, who are subject to daemonic power, shall utter their emotion in song, the musical burden is borne by the Saxon priests, the airy spirit Philidel, Grimbald, an Earthy Spirit, Cupid, Nymphs and Sylvans, Æolus, Comus, Venus and Honour whose only human attribute is her weakness for leading British heroes up the steepy height of Fame.

Critics of the drama seem to feel that there was something wilfully obstinate in the Restoration preference for the compromise of the dramatic or semi-opera. British musical historians tend, on their part, to account it a disgrace that Charles's musicians, in spite of the fact that they possessed the potential abilities, produced no *Pomo d'Oro* or *Armide*. We should reserve our condemnation until we have the good fortune to see and hear the best they offer in substitute. By 1690 the men of the theater knew well enough what could be attempted and what must be avoided in the musical drama. No genuine opera could at the time have been forced by such a categorical attitude as Motteux displays: "Other Nations bestow the name of Opera only on such Plays whereof every word is sung. But experience hath taught us that our English genius will not rellish that perpetual Singing. . . . Our English Gentlemen, when their Ear is satisfy'd, are desirous to have their mind pleas'd, and Music and Dancing industriously intermix'd with Comedy or Tragedy."[10]

How then, to revert to a question asked at the beginning of this excursion into the history of opera, did English taste suddenly desert the happy compromise and storm the doors of Drury Lane when *Arsinoe, Queen of Cyprus*, the first authentic Italian opera in English, opened in January 1705? Actually the change in taste was not quite so abrupt or pervasive as it is sometimes assumed to have been. The new vogue was not permanent nor very serious for the native ballad opera shortly succeeded it. Nor were the semi-operas entirely supplanted. *Macbeth*, with Leveridge's music, *The Emperor of the Moon,*

---

[9] *Albion and Albanius,* the Preface.

[10] *Gentleman's Journal.* January 1691/2. Fifteen years later, as one of the sponsors of Italian opera in English, Motteux was of a different mind.

*King Arthur* and the operatic *Tempest* continued in the repertory. It must also be observed that the marvellous performance of such native singers as Leveridge, Mrs. Cross and Mrs. Lindsey and their foreign rivals contributed as much to the success of the new ventures as the novelty of their matter and form.

The English public had agreed from the beginning of the period that the powers of inspiration were sufficiently strong to compel certain supernatural or semi-heroic persons to burst into song on the stage and their demand for these explosions in the regular drama as well as the dramatic operas was insatiable. But the realistic principle must always be followed. Priests in any part of the world might sing at their work of incantation and sacrifice. Witches and demons might howl to horrid music. Stereotyped scenes of this nature are presently to be expected as the fitting prelude to the climax in nearly every fourth act. Pagan ritual in Love's Temple fills the third and fourth acts of Flecknoe's *Love's Kingdom* (1664) and a sacrifice adorns the last act. Sir Robert Howard sacrifices in the Temple of the Sun in Act V of the *Indian Queen* (1664). The altar scene in *Sophonisba* (1675) requires the priestess of Bellona to struggle musically with the god. *Mithradates* (1678) opens in the outer part of the Temple of the Sun, with a "noise of Musick and tuning Voices." Mrs. Behn contributes to the ethnological history of North America by the scene of Indian ceremonial in Act IV of *The Widow Ranter* (1689). After the priests and priestesses have danced about their idol "with ridiculous postures," thrice repeated the mysterious incantation *Agah Yerkin, Agah Boah, Sulen Tawarapah,* "they sing something fine." In Dryden's *Oedipus* (?1692) Tiresias invokes the ghost of Laius after the "voices" have uttered

> such sounds as Hell ne'er heard,
> Since *Orpheus* brib'd the Shades.

Another means of avoiding the operatic conventions while satisfying the longing for musical interludes was found in the masque. This sort of entertainment was, of course, traditional and therefore acceptable on the English stage. In a sense, too, it conformed to the requirement of realism for in an era which carried on its intrigues under the cover of masquerade, the plotting which proceeded behind masques on the stage was not very different from the procuring which went on behind vizards in box and pit. Charles could not afford the gorgeous masques which his mother had so delighted in. *Calisto: or, the Chaste Nymph* (1675) in which he indulged for the sake of his queen, must have brought effective protests from the harassed guardians of his treasury. But the public stage which had in earlier days followed the court in these matters afar off, willingly took over the task of the invention of masques for both audiences.

To reckon up the number of masque scenes in Restoration drama would make a tedious tale. In 1663 Sir Robert Stapylton devoted one to Apollo in Act III of *The Stepmother* and another to Diana in Act IV. As late as 1696 Cibber could find no better way of ending his epochal *Love's Last Shift* than with a masque of Love, Honor and Reason. In the course of forty years some scenes of extraordinary beauty, like the little masque or interlude of nymphs and shepherds in Shadwell's *Libertine*, were brought to birth. The height is reached in Purcell's *Fairy Queen* (1692) in which, as Professor Dent says, "the masque is developed to such an extent as to absorb practically the whole of the music."[11]

The rest of the incidental music in the Restoration theater is as faithful a transcript from life as is, to a large extent, the drama which it embellishes. The tavern catches, serenading songs, the musical preludes to seduction, the soft airs to the lute sung to quiet the suffering heart, the healths to majesty, the musical performing of witty servants had their counterpart in society. The waits were still familiar figures in the London streets, and servants offered among their qualifications their skill in reading a part at sight. One remembers what Pepys says of his page: "a brave boy, sings finely, and is the most pleasant boy at present, while his ignorant boys's tricks last, that ever I saw."

To men like Roger North and John Dryden (before he succumbed to the genius of Purcell), purists in music and the drama, the artistic hybrids of the day doubtless gave pain. What Shadwell wrote of the ordinary theater composers was to them the sad truth about the whole tribe.

> Still in their Beaten Road, they troll along,
> And make alike the sad and cheerful Song:
> The Past'ral, and the War-like are the same;
> The Dirge, and Triumph, differ but in Name . . .
> A Funeral Song they Chaunt with cheerful Mood,
> And Sigh and Languish in a Drunken Ode.
> In Martial ones they're soft, in Am'rous rough;
> And never think they Shake and Grace enough.[12]

To the pleasure-seekers who composed the audience their new delight in a musical theater hardly needed explanation or excuse. If they had been pressed to a justification, they would probably have fallen back on the general argument which D'Avenant had first proposed. If tragedy can be raised above the common dialect by the refinement of the language so that the passions will rise with the height of the verse, then

> Vocal Musick adds new wings to all
> The flights of Poetry.
> *Playhouse to be Let, c.* 1662

*   *   *

A word of explanation is due in regard to the choice of songs in this volume. I have tried in the first place to represent the varieties of their use in the drama, exclusive of the opera. The composers were selected mainly on the ground of their intimate connection with the theater

---

[11] *Foundations*, p. 225.
[12] "To . . . Signior Pietro Reggio, on the Publishing his Book of Songs."

rather than their chance employment there. If the excellence of the music had been the chief consideration, Purcell would have to dominate in a group including possibly only Humphrey, Banister, King, Courteville and Daniel Purcell. The two songs of Shadwell are here because they have not been noticed before and because his love of music and his encouragement of the musico-dramatic mongrels demand that he be given a place. Songs by Leveridge and Mountfort find their place because the composers were actors and their songs represent the popular level of theater music.

To those for whom the vagaries of seventeenth century musical notation will be too puzzling to cope with easily, the poems are offered as consolation. None has been admitted unless it could pass the test of topical interest or intrinsic value. There would have been more of Dryden if Mr. Day had not forestalled me with his scholarly and finely appreciative *Songs of John Dryden*. As with Purcell, however, to allow Dryden to dominate the scene would be to risk a distortion of the whole picture.

In searching for the songs I have necessarily followed the quarry in many libraries. I am indebted for assistance in the hunt to the authorities at the New York Public Library, the Library of Congress, the Folger Library, the Harvard University Library, the British Museum, the Bodleian, Chetham's Library of Manchester, the Royal College of Music, the Library of Christ Church. I am obligated to the Reference Librarian at Princeton for negotiating the loan of books for me and to Mr. Strickland Gibson of the Bodleian for running down a MS. of Anthony à Wood to which musicologists had made vague but tantalizing references. I wish especially to acknowledge my debt to Professor G. H. Gerould of Princeton who graciously read the book in manuscript and made valuable suggestions for its betterment.

The portraits of Henry Purcell and Captain Pack are reproduced by courtesy of the Trustees of the British Museum.

I ask that the American Council of Learned Societies, which appointed me to a fellowship for 1931-1932, at which time this book was begun, will accept it as a partial fulfilment of the confidence they had in me. Finally I should like my readers to be aware of my gratitude to the Council of the Humanities at Princeton for their assumption of a share of the costs of its publication.

# JOHN DRYDEN

## THE INDIAN EMPEROUR,
### OR,
## THE CONQUEST OF MEXICO BY THE SPANIARDS (1665)

The Spaniards are enjoying a little idyllic interlude in their conquest of Mexico. The scene opens in a pleasant Grotto: "*in it a Fountain spouting; round about it* Vasquez, Pizzaro, *and other* Spaniards *lying carelesly un-arm'd, and by them many* Indian *Women, one of which Sings the following Song.*" The song finished, two Spaniards dance a "Saraband *with* Castanieta's" at the end of which the Indians make a surprise attack.

*Ah fading joy, how quickly art thou past?*
*Yet we thy ruine haste:*
*As if the cares of Humane Life were few*
*We seek out new:*
*And follow Fate that does too fast pursue.*

*See how on every bough the Birds express*
*In their sweet notes their happiness.*
*They all enjoy, and nothing spare;*
*But on their Mother Nature lay their care:*
*Why then should Man, the Lord of all below*
*Such troubles chuse to know*
*As none of all his Subjects undergo?*

*Hark, hark, the Waters fall, fall, fall;*
*And with a Murmuring sound*
*Dash, dash, upon the ground,*
*To gentle slumbers call.*
(1667, Act IV, Scene 3)[1]

[1] The date at the beginning of each song is the year of the play's production; the date at the end indicates the year of the first quarto from which the text of the song as here printed is taken. The attempt has been made to reproduce the typography of the quartos. The text of the music is in each instance the first printing unless otherwise stated in the notes, where bibliographical details are given.

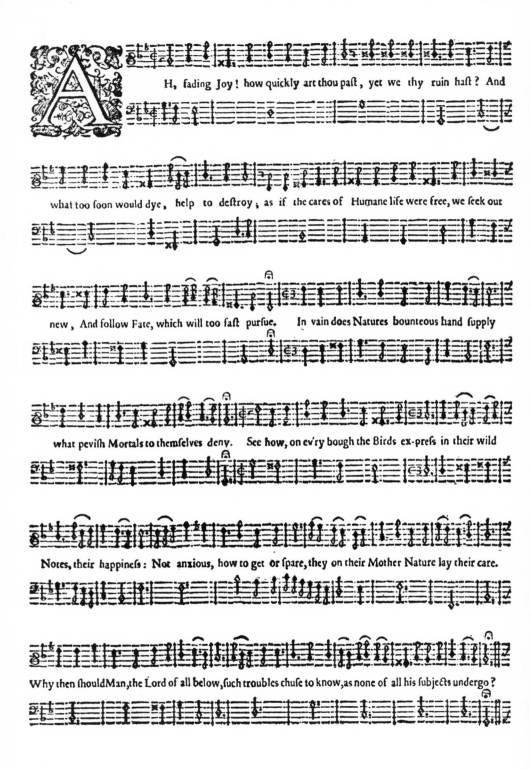

A H, fading Joy! how quickly art thou paſt, yet we thy ruin haſt? And

what too ſoon would dye, help to deſtroy, as if the cares of Humane life were free, we ſeek out

new, And follow Fate, which will too faſt purſue. In vain does Natures bounteous hand ſupply

what peviſh Mortals to themſelves deny. See how, on ev'ry bough the Birds ex-preſs in their wild

Notes, their happineſs: Not anxious, how to get or ſpare, they on their Mother Nature lay their care.

Why then ſhouldMan, the Lord of all below, ſuch troubles chuſe to know, as none of all his ſubjects undergo?

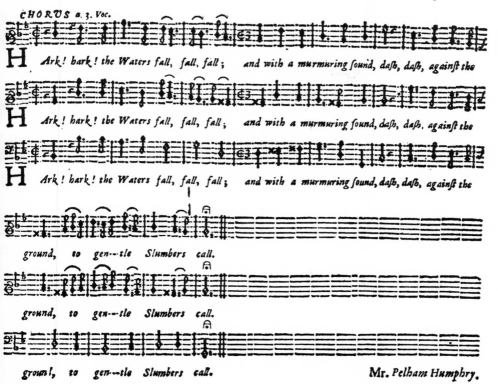

*CHORUS a. 3. Voc.*

Hark! hark! the Waters fall, fall, fall; and with a murmuring sound, dash, dash, against the

Hark! hark! the Waters fall, fall, fall; and with a murmuring sound, dash, dash, against the

Hark! hark! the Waters fall, fall, fall; and with a murmuring sound, dash, dash, against the

ground, to gen---tle Slumbers call.

ground, to gen---tle Slumbers call.

ground, to gen---tle Slumbers call.

Mr. Pelham Humphry.

JOHN CROWNE

JULIANA
OR
THE PRINCESS OF POLAND (1671)

The wretched Paulina describes her own unhappy situation: "Marry a Lady o' my quality, and then deny the marriage! oh perfidious ungrateful man! and was it then for this [I] trampled on my self, my Honors, Fortunes, run on the pikes of my great Fathers anger, bestow'd thy life, when all thy friends abandon'd thee, and for thy sake am now become a poor and wandring Exile; and thou thus reward me, basely abandon me? oh horrid, horrid, weep, bleed, die, fall at my feet thou Tyrant. . . ." It is all a bad mistake. She had, true enough, helped the hero to escape and she now pursues him in disguise. Yet it was not he, as we know all the time, but the Prince Demetrius who betrayed her into a false marriage. The play opens in a grove: "Paulina *sleeping under a Tree*; Joanna *sitting by and singing.*"

L O, behind a Scene of Seas,
  *Under a Canopy of Trees,*
   *The fair new Golden World was laid;*
   *Sleeping like a naked Maid,*
   *Till alas! she was betray'd:*
  *In such shades* Urania *lay,*
*Till Love discover'd out a way:*
*And now she cries some Power above,*
*Save me from this Tyrant Love.*

*Her poor heart had no defence,*
*But its Maiden Innocence;*
  *In each sweet retiring Eye,*
  *You might easily descry*
  *Troops of yielding Beauties flye,*
*Leaving Rare unguarded Treasure*
*To the Conquerors will and pleasure:*
*And now she cries, ———— &c.*

*Now and then a stragling frown,*
*Through the shades skipt up and down;*
  *Shooting such a piercing Dart,*
  *As would make the Tyrant smart,*
  *And preserve her Lips, and Heart.*
*But, alas! her Empire's gone,*
*Thrones and Temples all undone:*
*And now she cryes ———— &c.*

*Charm aloft the stormy Winds,*
*That may keep these Golden Mines,*
  *And let Spaniard Love be tore*
  *On some cruel Rocky Shore,*
  *Where he'l put to Sea no more;*
*Lest poor conquer'd Beauty cry,*
*Oh! I'm wounded! oh! I dye!*
*And there is no power above*
*Saves me from this Tyrant love.*

(1671, Act I, Scene 1)

O behind a Scene of Seas, under a Canopy of Trees; The fair new golden world was laid sleeping, like a harmless Maid, 'till alas, she was betray'd: In such shades Urania lay, 'till Love discover'd out a way; And now she cryes, Some pow'r above, save me from this Tyrant Love.

Mr. *John Banister*.

II.
Her poor Heart had no defence,
But its Maiden innocence ;
In each sweet retyring eye,
You might easily discry
Troops of yielding beauties fly,
Leaving rare unguarded treasure
To the Conquerors will and pleasure.
    And now she cryes , &c.

III.
Now and then, a straggling frown,
( Through the shade flips up and down )
Shooting such a piercing dart,
As would make the Tyrant smart ,
And preserve Her Lips and Heart :
But alas, her Empires gone ,
Throne, and Temples, all undone.
    And now she cryes, &c.

IV.
Charm aloft, those stormy winds,
That may keep these Golden Mines ;
And let *Spaniards* Love be tore
On some cruel Rocky shore ,
Where he'll put forth to Sea no more :
Least poor conquered Beauty cry ,
Oh, I'm wounded! Oh, I dye !
    And then, there is no pow'r above
    Can save me from this Tyrant Love.

## WILLIAM WYCHERLEY

### LOVE IN A WOOD,
OR,
### ST. JAMES'S PARK (1671)

Lady Flippant, though in distress for a husband, rails against marriage to make the fops more eager. Ranger has rambled within her preserves, and she manages to hold him for a moment with this song of which she admits "though it be the fashion for women of quality to sing any Song whatever, because the words are not distinguish'd; yet I should have blush'd to have done it now, but for you, Sir." Ranger finds the song edifying and the voice admirable. It was to the last line of this song that the Duchess of Cleveland referred when she thrust herself out of her chariot in the Mall to shout at the witty young author, "You, Wycherley, you are a Son of a Whore." He pursued and persuaded her to see the play where she sat in the front row of the King's box while he entertained her from the pit below.

*A Spouse I do hate,*
*For either she's false or she's jealous;*
*But give us a Mate,*
*Who nothing will ask us, or tell us.*

*She stands on no terms,*
*Nor chaffers, by way of Indenture,*
*Her love for your Farms;*
*But takes her kind man at a venture.*

*If all prove not right,*
*Without an Act, Process, or Warning,*
*From Wife for a night,*
*You may be divorc'd in the morning.*

*When Parents are Slaves,*
*Their Bratts cannot be any other;*
*Great Wits, and great Braves,*
*Have always a Punk to their Mother.*

(1672, Act I, Scene 2)

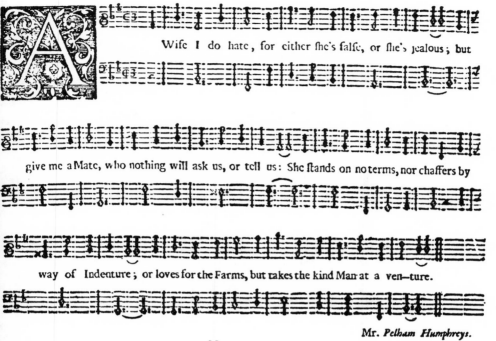

Wife I do hate, for either she's false, or she's jealous; but give me a Mate, who nothing will ask us, or tell us: She stands on no terms, nor chaffers by way of Indenture; or loves for the Farms, but takes the kind Man at a ven—ture.

Mr. *Pelham Humphreys.*

II.

If all prove not right,
Without an Act, Process or warning,
From Wife for a night,
You may be divorc'd the next morning.
Where Parents are Slaves,
Their Brats cann't be any other;
Great Wits and great Braves
Have always a Punk to their Mother.

## JOHN DRYDEN

### Marriage A-la-Mode (1672)

Doralice has grown weary of her new husband Rhodophil, the Captain of the Guards, at the exact moment when his witty friend Palamede comes home from his travels. You will imagine what follows, though not as much follows as you will imagine. This can be said for Palamede, if anything must be said at all: no one had troubled to inform him of the marriage. When the first scene is opened Doralice and Beliza retire into the arbor with a lute. Palamede overhears their song and begins his campaign with a pretty compliment to the singers: "I thought good voices, and ill faces, had been inseparable; and that to be fair and sing well, had been onely the priviledge of Angels."

I.

W*Hy should a foolish Marriage Vow*
     *Which long ago was made,*
*Oblige us to each other now*
     *When Passion is decay'd?*
*We lov'd, and we lov'd, as long as we cou'd,*
     *Till our love was lov'd out in us both:*
*But our Marriage is dead, when the Pleasure is fled:*
     *'Twas Pleasure first made it an Oath.*

2.

*If I have Pleasures for a Friend,*
     *And farther love in store,*
*What wrong has he whose joys did end,*
     *And who cou'd give no more?*

*'Tis a madness that he*
*Should be jealous of me,*
*Or that I shou'd bar him of another:*
*For all we can gain,*
*Is to give our selves pain,*
*When neither can hinder the other.*

(1673, Act I, Scene 1)

Hy ſhould a fooliſh Marriage Vow, which long agoe was made, abligé us to each other now, when paſſion is de-cay'd? We loved and lov'd, as long as we could, 'till our Love was lov'd out of us both. But the Marriage is dead, when the pleaſure is fled; 'twas pleaſure firſt made it an Oath.

Mr. *Robert Smith.*

II.

If I have pleaſure for a friend,
And further joy in ſtore,
What wrong has he whoſe joys did end,
And who could give no more?
It's a madneſs that he
Should be jealous of me,
Or that I ſhould bar him of another,
When all we can gain
Is to give our ſelves pain,
And neither can hinder the other.

## WILLIAM WYCHERLEY

### THE GENTLEMAN DANCING-MASTER (1672)

Hippolita is a young lady who takes matters into her own hands. She will have Gerrard to a husband in spite of the tyrannical commands of her father that she marry her foppish cousin newly arrived from Paris with a new outfit and a new suit of manners. And Hippolita resolves to take her lover while she has him. That is why she particularly liked this song and welcomed the gentlewoman from the next house when she consented to perform it again for her. 'Tis "the new Song against delays in Love."

1.

*Since we poor slavish Women know*
*Our men we cannot pick and choose,*
*To him we like, why say we no?*
*And both our time and Lover lose.*

*With feign'd repulses and delays*
*A Lovers appetite we pall;*
*And if too long the Gallant stays,*
*His stomach's gone for good and all.*

2.

*Or our impatient am'rous Guest,*
*Unknown to us, away may steal,*
*And rather than stay for a Feast,*
*Take up with some coorse, ready meal.*

*When opportunity is kind,*
*Let prudent Woman be so too;*
*And if the man be to your mind,*
*Till needs you must, ne're let him go.*

3.

*The Match soon made is happy still,*
*For only Love has there to do;*
*Let no one marry 'gainst her will,*
*But stand off, when her Parents woo.*

*And only to their Suits be coy,*
*For she whom Joynter can obtain*
*To let a Fop her Bed enjoy,*
*Is but a lawful Wench for gain.*

(1673, Act II, Scene 1)

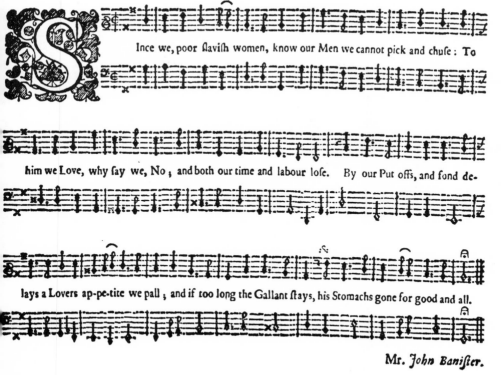

Ince we, poor flavifh women, know our Men we cannot pick and chufe : To

him we Love, why fay we, No ; and both our time and labour lofe.    By our Put offs, and fond de-

lays a Lovers ap-pe-tite we pall ; and if too long the Gallant ftays, his Stomachs gone for good and all.

Mr. *John Banifter.*

### II.

Or our impatient Amorous gueſt ,
Unknown to us away may ſteal ;
And rather then ſtay for a feaſt ,
Take up with ſome courſe ready meal.
When opportunity is kind ,
Let prudent Women be ſo to ;
And if the Man be to her mind ,
Be ſure ſhe do not let him go.

### III.

The Match ſoon made, is happieſt ſtill ,
For Love has only there to do :
Let no one Marry 'gainſt her will ,
But ſtand off when her Parents woo :
And to the Suror be not coy ;
For they whom Joynture can obtain ,
To let a Fop her Bed enjoy ,
Is but a lawful Wench for gain.

## APHRA BEHN

### THE DUTCH LOVER (1672/3)

Hippolyta is one of those Behnian heroines who like to be abused by men and enjoy complaining of their difficulties even more. She has suffered enough from Antonio to drive a less pliant lady quite out of her head, but she has not nearly endured all when she sings this song in the third act. Though Antonio has, it is true, betrayed and ravished her, that is only the beginning. The direction reads: "*Draws off, discovers* Antonio *sleeping on the ground*; Hippolyta *sitting by, who sings*."

A H false Amyntas, *can that hour*
*So soon forgotten be,*
*When first I yielded up my power*
*To be betray'd by thee?*
*God knows with how much innocence*
*I did my heart resign,*
*Unto thy faithless eloquence,*
*And gave thee what was mine.*

*I had not one reserve in store,*
*But at thy feet I laid*
*Those arms which conquer'd heretofore,*
*Though now thy trophies made.*
*Thy eyes in silence told their tale,*
*Of love in such a way,*
*That 'twas as easie to prevail,*
*As after to betray.*

(1673, Act III, Scene 3)

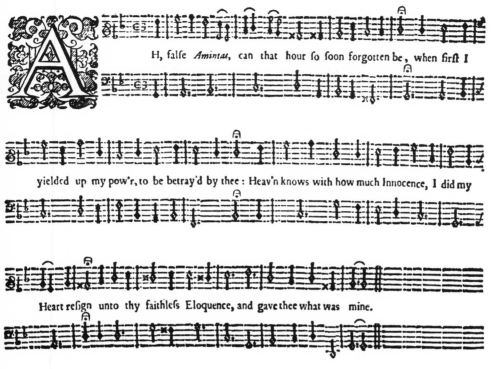

H, falſe *Amintas*, can that hour ſo ſoon forgotten be, when firſt I yielded up my pow'r, to be betray'd by thee : Heav'n knows with how much Innocence, I did my Heart reſign unto thy faithleſs Eloquence, and gave thee what was mine.

Mr. *Robert Smith.*

### II.

I had not one Reſerve in ſtore,
But at thy feet I lay'd
Thoſe arms that conquer'd heretofore,
Though now thy Trophies made :
Thy Eyes in ſilence told their Tale
Of Love in ſuch a way,
That 'twas as eaſie to prevail,
As after to betray.

## NATHANIEL LEE

Sophonisba,

OR

Hannibal's Overthrow (1675)

Hannibal has sought the priestesses of Bellona to learn his fate in war and love. Cumana, the second priestess, is preparing for prophecy within.

> Full of the Deity, about she roams
> Stares, gapes, and on the hallow'd Curtains foams;
> Cuts her hot Flesh, grovels upon the Ground
> Sings, dances, kicks the golden Tripods round.

We are denied a sight of these diverting preliminaries. When she appears on the scene to deliver her prophecy, the fury has subsided and she is merely scratching her face and stabbing a dagger into her arms while the spirits follow her about. The scene is one of the numerous imitations of Macbeth's midnight visit to the hags which a Restoration dramatist could rely on to conceal the weakness of his fourth act.

> *Beneath the Poplar's shaddow lay me,*
> *No raging fires will there dismay me.*
> *Near some silver current lying,*
> *Under sleepy Poppies dying.*
> *I swell, and am bigger than* Typhon *e're was,*
> *With a strong band of Brass, O bind me about;*
> *Least my bosome should burst for the secret to pass:*
> *And a vent being given the fury get out.*
> *I cannot, I will not be vext any longer,*
> *While I rage I grow weak, and the Goddess grows stronger.*
> (1676, Act IV, Scene 1)

# A *Mad* SONG.

Beneath a Poplar's shadow lay me, no ra . . . . . . . . . . . ging Fires will there dif-

—may me; near some silver Current lying, near some silver Current lying; Oh! oh! under

slee——py Poppies dying: I swell——and am bigger, I swell

. . . . . . . and am bigger than *Typhon* e're was; with a strong band of Brass oh! bind me, oh!

bind me about! left my Bosom shou'd burst, for the secret to pass, and the Fu . . . . . . . . ry get out,

I cannot, I will not, I cannot, I will not be vex't any longer, while I ra . . . . . .

. . . . . ge I grow weak, while I ra . . . . . . . . . . . . ge, while I ra . . . . . . . .

—ge I grow weak, and the Goddess grows stronger.

## NATHANIEL LEE

GLORIANA,

OR

THE COURT OF AUGUSTUS CAESAR (1675/6)

Augustus Caesar, whose amours should have ended long ago, has so far fallen in love with Gloriana that he threatens to come to her by moonlight, like Tarquin "pale resolv'd upon the Deed." This song, which is sung in Gloriana's bower just before Caesar enters "with all violence of mind" to woo her, suggests, in an unheroic key, the theme of the play.

1.

*AH the charms of a Beauty disdainfull and fair,*
*How she blasts all my joys when she bids me despair:*
*Forgetting my State, when I sigh and lye down,*
*And cast at her feet both Scepter and Crown,*
*She passes regardless, and says a young Swain,*
*Before an old Monarch, her love should obtain.*

2.

*Remember, Fair Nymph, my Grandfather* Jove,
*That rev'rend old God always made the best Love:*
*So fiercely he mov'd with a manner Divine,*
*That he melted his way, or blew up the Mine.*
*Your scorn of my age therefore cease to pursue,*
*And think what a loving old* Caesar *can do.*

(1676, Act III, Scene 2)

H, the Charms of a Beauty, difdainful and fair, how fhe blafts all my

Joys, when fhe bids me defpair; forgetting my State, when I Sigh and lye down, and caft at her

Feet both Scepter and Crown; She paffes regardlefs, and fays, A young Swain, before an old

Monarch her Love fhould obtain.

II.

Forbear, my *Gloriana*, to laugh at my Age,
Nor think me lefs apt than the Young, to engage;
Though the Politick States-man in care fpends the Light,
He puts off his troubles, and laughs all the Night:
He wakes like a Star, ever fixt to his Sphear;
And his Miftrefs looks pale, when the Morning draws near.

THOMAS DURFEY

POETA LYRICUS.

## THOMAS D'URFEY

### A FOND HUSBAND:
#### OR,
### THE PLOTTING SISTERS (1677)

Bubble, the willing wittol of D'Urfey's play, hires a poet to make this song in praise of lawful love especially for a little party he gives in honor of his wife's virtue. The poet had to labor over it because he had nothing in stock at all like it. The town loves and demands nothing but satires against marriage. This song is in quite a new vein.

U*Nder the Branches of a spreading Tree,*
  Silvander *sate, from care and danger free,*
*And his inconstant roving humour shows*
*To his dear Nymph, that sung of Marriage-Vows:*
*But she with flowing Graces charming Air,*
  *Cry'd, Fie, fie, my Dear, give o'er,*
  *Ah, tempt the gods no more!*
*But thy offence with penitence repair:*
*For though Vice in a Beauty seem sweet in thy Arms,*
*An Innocent Virtue has always more Charms.*

2.

*Ah* Phillida! *the angry Swain reply'd,*
*Is not a Mistriss better than a Bride?*
*What Man that Universal Yoke retains,*
*But meets an hour to sigh and curse his chains?*
*She smiling cry'd, Change, change that impious Mind;*
*Without it we could prove not half the Joys of Love.*
*'Tis Marriage makes the feeling Joys Divine:*
*For all our Life long we from scandal remove,*
*And at last fall the Trophies of Honour and Love.*
            (1677, Act IV, Scene 2)

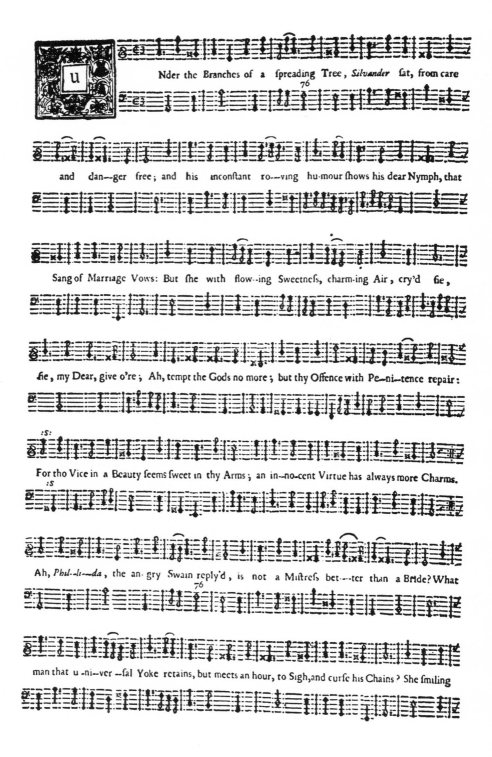

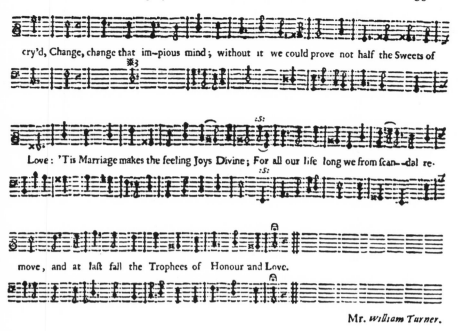

cry'd, Change, change that im‑pious mind; without it we could prove not half the Sweets of

Love : 'Tis Marriage makes the feeling Joys Divine; For all our life long we from scan‑ ‑dal re‑

move , and at laſt fall the Trophees of Honour and Love.

Mr. *William Turner.*

## NAHUM TATE

### BRUTUS OF ALBA:
#### OR,
### THE ENCHANTED LOVERS (1678)

The story of Brutus of Alba and the Queen of Syracuse is the tale of Dido and Aeneas transformed to suit the Restoration taste. This demanded that the adulterous passion of the hero and heroine should be haunted at crucial moments by the ghosts of their former spouses. Brutus's agony in having to choose between his love for the Queen and the plain duty of founding the British Empire is in the correct heroic mode. When he departs the Queen goes distracted. Her confidante, who knows what is good for such cases, orders a song:

> Soft Musick, and complaining Songs may calm
> This Rage, I've known it a successfull Charm.

> *Bid the sad forsaken Grove*
> *To sigh for ever, sigh as much as I.*
> *Bid the Dew fall, and the Skie weep apace,*
> > *Weep like the Queen of Love:*
> *It cannot be more show'ry then her Face.*
> > *Ah hapless Deity,*
> *And still more wretched 'cause she may not Die.*
> *Can there be further joy in the Celestial store,*
> *Now my best Heav'n Adonis is no more,*
> *He is no more, no more!*

> *Hark, methinks I hear each Tree*
> *Murmur in Parts as sighing Breezes rise*
> *And make (whilst Time their nodding Branches keep)*
> > *A mournfull Symphony.*
> *The Skies to find a thousand Eyes to weep.*
> > *Ah you deceitfull Skies,*
> *When my Adonis fell where were those Eyes?*
> *Can there be further joy in the Celestial store,*
> *Since the sweet Youth Adonis is no more,*
> *He is no more, &c.*

Wright (1678, Act V, Scene 2)

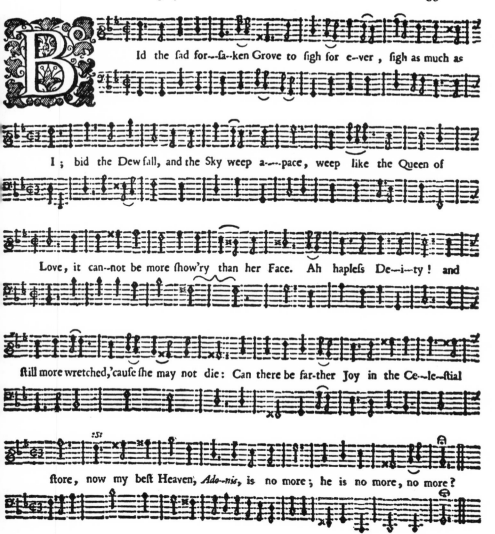

Id the sad for---sa--ken Grove to sigh for e--ver , sigh as much as

I ;  bid the Dew fall, and the Sky weep a----pace, weep  like the Queen of

Love, it can--not be more show'ry than her Face.  Ah haples De---i--ty ! and

still more wretched,'caufe she may not  die:  Can there be far-ther Joy in the Ce--le--ftial

store,  now  my beft Heaven, *Ado--nis,* is  no more ;  he is no more, no more?

Mr. *Farmer.*

## THOMAS D'URFEY

THE VIRTUOUS WIFE;

OR,

GOOD LUCK AT LAST (1679)

The song which Letitia sings at Sir Frolic's request has nothing to do with the action of D'Urfey's early sentimental comedy about a wronged wife who brings her husband to his senses without compromising her own honesty. It is one of innumerable "Scotch" songs which were written to sustain the vogue of sophisticated rusticity to which the Restoration pastoral also belongs. D'Urfey supplied the theater with many of these pseudo-Scotch ballads in his own plays and those of his friends.

1.

S Awney *was tall, and of noble Race,*
*And lov'd me better then any yen,*
But *noo he liggs by another Lasse,*
*And* Sawney *will nere be my Love agen.*
*I gave him a fine Scotch Sarke and Band,*
*I put um on with my awn hand;*
*I gave him House, and I gave him Land,*
*Yet* Sawney *will ne'ere be my Love agen.*

2.

*I rob'd the Groves of all their Store,*
*And Nosegayes made to give* Sawney *yen;*
*He kist my Breast, and fain would do more,*
*Gude feth methought he was a bonny yen:*
*He squeez'd my Fingers, grasp'd my Knee,*
*And Carv'd my name on each green Tree;*
*And sigh'd and languisht to ligg by me;*
*But now he ne'ere will be my Love agen.*

3.

*My Bongrace, and my Sun-burnt Face*
*He prais'd; and also my Russet Gown;*
*But now he dotes on the Copper Lace,*
*Of some lew'd Quean of* London-*Town.*
*He gangs and gives her Curds and Creame,*
*Whilst I poor Saule sit sighing at heam;*
*And ne're Joye* Sawney *unless in a Dreame;*
*For now he ne're will be my Love agen.*

(1680, Act III, Scene 1)

# A NORTHERN SONG.

Aw--ney was tall, and of no--ble Race, and lov'd me bet--ter than

a--ny yen; but now he ligs by a--no--ther Lass, and Saw--ney, ne're be my Love a--gen.

I gave him a fine *Scoch* Sark and Band, I put them on with mine own hand; I

gave him a House, I gave him Land, yet *Saw--ney* will ne're be my Love a--gen.

**II.**

I robb'd the Groves of all their Store,
And Nosegays made to give *Sawney* one;
He kiss'd my Brest, and fain would do more,
Gude Feth, me thought he was a bonny one.
He squeez'd my Fingers, grasp'd my Knee,
And carv'd my Name on each green Tree;
Sigh'd and languish'd to ligg by me,
But now he will ne're be my Love agen.

**III.**

My Boongrace, and my Sun-burnt Face,
He prais'd, and also my Russet Gown;
But now he dotes on the Copper Lace
Of some lewd Queen of *LONDON* Town.
He gangs and gives her Curds and Cream,
Whil'st I poor Soul sit sighing at heam;
I ne're joy *Sawney* unless in a Dream,
For now he will ne're be my Love agen.

## THOMAS OTWAY

### THE ORPHAN:
OR,
### THE UNHAPPY-MARRIAGE (1680)

Otway's tragedy presents one of those insolvable ethical situations which were then the chief requirement of a serious play. Castalio and Polydore, twins and sworn friends, both love Monimia, the orphan ward of their father. Castalio has secretly married her but plays his brother false by not telling him. Polydore overhears their arrangement for an assignation and, supposing it illicit, usurps Castalio's place. Refused admittance to his wife's chamber, Castalio is wild with anger. At the beginning of Act V he is discovered lying on the ground listening to this song. When Polydore learns what an unatonable thing he has done, he contrives to make his brother kill him. Monimia dies of self-accusation and Castalio stabs himself.

C*Ome, all ye Youths, whose Hearts e're bled*
　　*By cruel Beauties Pride,*
*Bring each a Garland on his head*
　　*Let none his Sorrows hide,*
*But hand in hand around me move*
　　*Singing the saddest Tales of Love;*
　　　　*And see, when your Complaints ye joyn,*
　　　　*If all your Wrongs can equal mine.*

2.

*The happyest Mortal once was I,*
　　*My heart no Sorrows knew.*
*Pity the Pain with which I dye,*
　　*But ask not whence it grew.*
*Yet if a tempting Fair you find*
　　*That's very lovely, very kind,*
　　　　*Though bright as Heaven whose stamp she bears,*
　　　　*Think of my Fate, and shun her Snares.*
　　　　　　　　(1680, Act V, Scene 1)

Ome all the Youths, whose Hearts have bled by cru---el Beau-ties

Pride; bring each a Garland on his Head, let none his Sorrows hide:

But hand in hand a round me move, singing the sad---dest Tales of Love; and

try when your Complaints ye joyn, if all your wrongs can e---qual mine.

Mr. *Fran. Forcer.*

II.
The happ'est Mortal once was I,
My Heart no Sorrow knew;
Pity the Pain with which I dye,
But ask not whence it grew:

Yet if a Tempting fair you find
That's very lovely, very kind;
Though bright as Heaven, whose Stamp she bear,
Think of my Fate, and shun her Snare.

From an engraving, "The Portsmouth Captains," by R. White, 1688

# THOMAS SOUTHERNE

## THE DISAPPOINTMENT

### OR

## THE MOTHER IN FASHION (1684)

Alphonso who wrongly suspects his wife Erminia of granting favors to Alberto obliges her to permit him an assignation, the innocence of which he intends to judge while hidden in the next room. This melting song in praise of illicit love Alberto sings to Erminia as an aphrodisiac. Its seductive cadences and the impassioned addresses of Alberto which ensue have nearly fatal consequences.

*SEe how fair* Corinna *lies,*
   *Kindly calling with her Eyes:*
*In the tender Minute prove her;*
Shepherd! *Why so dull a Lover?*
*Prithee, Why so dull a Lover?*

*In her blushes see your shame;*
*Anger they with Love proclaim;*
*You too coldly entertain her:*
*Lay your Pipe a little by,*
*If no other Charms you try,*
*You will never, never gain her.*

*While the happy Minute is,*
*Court her, you may get a kiss,*
*May be, favours that are greater:*
*Leave your Piping, to her fly,*
*When the* Nymph *you love is nigh,*
*Is it with a Tune you treat her?*

*Dull* Amintor! *fy, Oh! fy:*
*Now your* Shepherdess *is nigh;*
*Can you pass your time no better?*
      *Enter* Alberto.

*Alb.* So the kind *Nymph,* dissolving as she lay,
Expecting sigh'd, and chid the *Shepherds* stay:
When panting to the Joy, he flew, to prove
The Immortality of Life and Love.
        Sir George Etherege (1684, Act V, Scene 2)

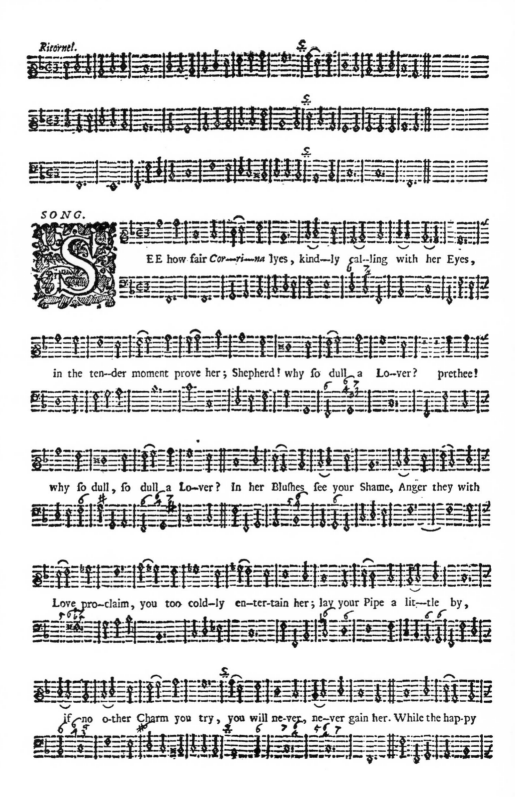

*Ritornel.*

*SONG.*

SEE how fair *Cor—ri—na* lyes, kind—ly cal—ling with her Eyes,

in the ten—der moment prove her; Shepherd! why so dull a Lo—ver? prethee!

why so dull, so dull a Lo—ver? In her Blushes see your Shame, Anger they with

Love pro—claim, you too cold—ly en—ter—tain her; lay your Pipe a lit—tle by,

if no o—ther Charm you try, you will ne—ver, ne—ver gain her. While the hap—py

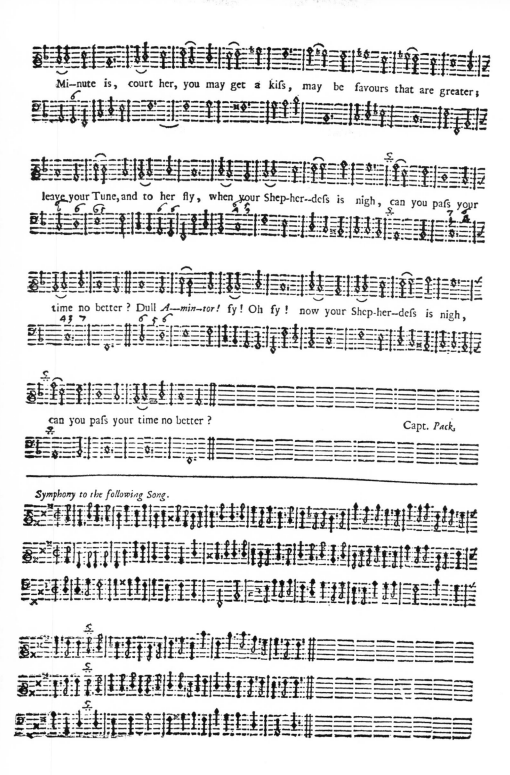

Mi—nute is, court her, you may get a kifs, may be favours that are greater;

leave your Tune, and to her fly, when your Shep-her--defs is nigh, can you pafs your

time no better? Dull A—min—tor! fy! Oh fy! now your Shep-her--defs is nigh,

can you pafs your time no better?

Capt. *Pack.*

*Symphony to the following Song.*

## NAHUM TATE

### A DUKE AND NO DUKE (1684)

Tate borrowed from Cockain his plot of a usurping ·Duke transformed by a conjurer into the shape of the rightful possessor, but he made a play which was popular enough to last a century in various forms. This song was one of those which were used as incidental music between the acts. It has no connection with the plot.

*Tell me no more I am deceiv'd,*
   *While* Sylvia *seems so kind;*
*And takes such care to be believ'd,*
   *The Cheat I fear to find:*
*To flatter me, should Falshood lye*
   *Conceal'd in her soft Youth;*
*A thousand times I'd rather dye,*
   *Than see the unhappy Truth;*
*A thousand times I'd rather dye,*
   *Than see th'unhappy Truth.*

### II.

*My Love all Malice shall outbrave,*
   *Let Fops in Libels rail;*
*If she the Appearances will save,*
   *No Scandal can prevail:*
*She makes me think I have her Heart,*
   *How much for that is due?*
*Tho' she but act the tender part,*
   *The Joy she gives is true.*

                    Sir George Etherege (1685)

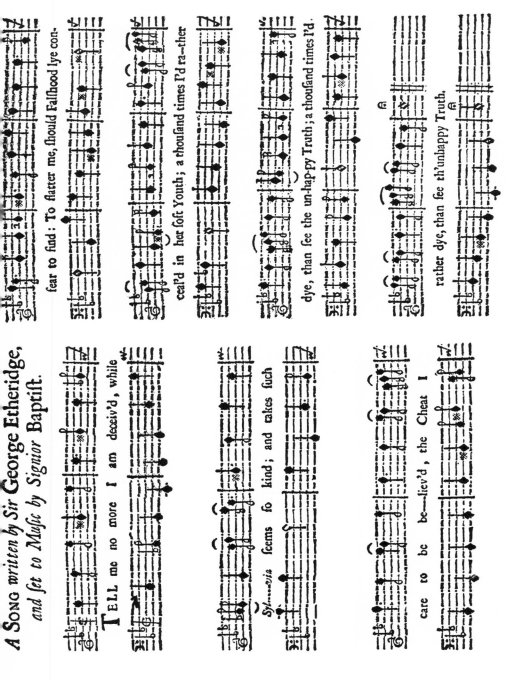

## NAHUM TATE

### CUCKOLDS-HAVEN:
#### OR,
### AN ALDERMAN NO CONJURER (1685)

The speaker of Tate's prologue is made to say:

*We own, nor to confess it are asham'd,*
*That from tough* Ben's *Remains, this Piece was fram'd.*

The "remains" were two plays, *Eastward Ho!* and *The Devil is an Ass*, which Tate squeezes together into three acts to make his farce. The part-song below has nothing to do with its action but was sung between Acts II and III as a compliment to King James who had just ascended the throne.

How great are the Blessings of Government made,
    *By the excellent Rule of our Prince?*
*Who, while Trouble and Cares do his Pleasures invade,*
    *To his People all Joy does dispense:*
*And while He for us is still carking and thinking,*
    *We have nothing to Mind, but our Shops and our Trade,*
       *And then to divert us with Drinking.*

*From him we derive all our Pleasure and Wealth:*
    *Then fill me a Glass, nay, fill it up higher,*
*My Soul is a thirst for His Majesty's Health,*
    *And an Ocean of Drink can't quench my Desire:*
*Since all we Enjoy, to his Bounty we Owe,*
*'Tis fit all our Bumpers like that shou'd O'reflow.*

(1685)

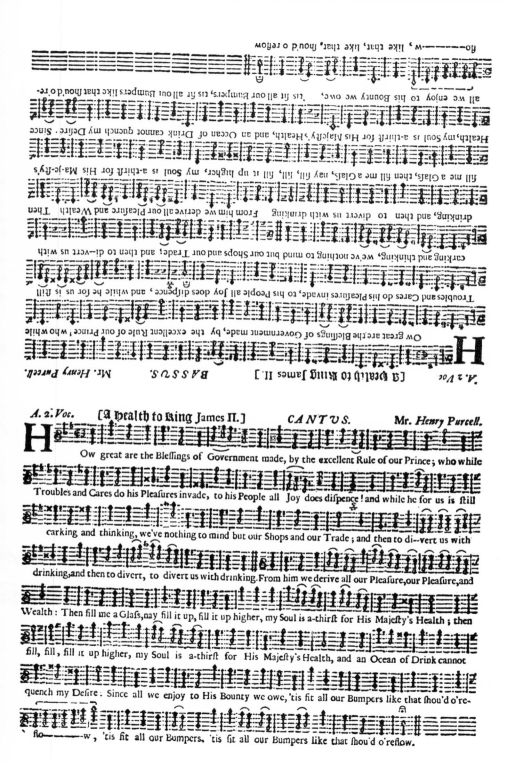

## SIR CHARLES SEDLEY

BELLAMIRA,

OR

THE MISTRESS (1687)

Thisbe has found a quiet moment and calls on her maid for the last new song. Though hotly pursued by Cunningham, who interrupts her as soon as the song is done, she has been proof against all advances. He has courted her six months, yet "never cou'd obtain the least indecent favour." Cunningham, so the tradition says, was intended for a portrait of Colonel Jack Churchill, afterwards the great Duke of Marlborough.

> Thyrsis *unjustly you Complain,*
> *And tax my tender heart*
> *With want of pity for your pain,*
> *Or Sense of your desert.*
>
> *By secret and Mysterious Springs,*
> *Alas! our Passions move;*
> *We Women are Fantastick things,*
> *That like before we love.*
>
> *You may be handsome, and have Wit,*
> *Be secret and well-bred,*
> *The Person Love must to us fit,*
> *He only can succeed.*
>
> *Some Dye, yet never are believ'd;*
> *Others we trust too soon,*
> *Helping ourselves to be deceiv'd,*
> *And proud to be undone.*

(1687, Act III, Scene 3)

A Song in *Bellamira*, or, the Miſtreſs.          Set by Mr. *Tho. Shadwell.*

*Hyrſis* un—juſt—ly you com—plain, and tax my tender heart, with want of pity for your pain , or ſence of your diſſert.

By ſecret and miſterious Springs alaſs our paſſions move, we Women are fan-taſtick things that like be—fore we love.

You may be handſome and have Wit,
    Be ſecret and well bred,
The Parſon Love muſt to us fit,
    He onely can ſucceed.
Some die and yet are ne're believ'd,
    Others we truſt too ſoon,
Helping our ſelves to be deceiv'd,
    And proud to be undone.

## THOMAS SHADWELL

### THE SQUIRE OF ALSATIA (1688)

Belfond Junior, who is as immoderately given to music as Shakespeare's Duke Orsino (whom he quotes), hides his new mistress with one hand while he ushers in his music master with the other. Solfa's daughter Betty sings "The Expostulation" for her employer.

### The Expostulation.

*Still wilt thou sigh, and still in vain*
*A cold neglectful Nymph adore;*
*No longer fruitlesly complain,*
*But to thy self thy self restore.*
*In Youth thou caught'st this fond disease,*
*And shouldst abandon it in age;*
*Some other Nymph as well may please,*
*Absence or bus'ness disingage.*

*On tender hearts the wounds of Love,*
*Like those imprinted on young Trees,*
*Or kill at first, or else they prove*
*Larger b' insensible degrees.*
*Business I try'd, she fill'd my mind;*
*On others Lips my Dear I kist;*
*But never solid Joy could find,*
*Where I my charming Sylvia mist.*

*Long Absence, like a Greenland night,*
*Made me but wish for Sun the more;*
*And that inimitable light,*
*She, none but she, could e'er restore.*
*She never once regards thy Fire,*
*Nor ever vents one sigh for thee.*
*I must the Glorious Sun admire,*
*Though he can never look on me.*

*Look well, you'll find she's not so rare,*
  *Much of her former Beauty's gone;*
*My Love her Shadow larger far*
  *Is made by her declining Sun.*
*What if her Glories faded be,*
  *My former wounds I must indure;*
*For should the Bow unbended be,*
  *Yet that can never help the Cure.*
                    (1688, Act II, Scene 1)

Till wilt thou ſigh and ſtill ---in----- vain a cold neg---lect--- full

Nymph a------dore, no longer fruitleſ----ly com---plain, but to thy-- ſelf--thy

ſelf re---ſto-----re : In Youth thou caught'ſt this fond diſ---caſe , and ſhould'ſt

abandon it in Age; ſome o--ther Nymph as well may pleaſe, ab---ſence or

buſi----neſs diſengage.

On tender hearts the wounds of Love,
Like thoſe imprinted on young Trees,
Or kill at firſt, or elſe they prove
Larger by inſenſible degrees.
Buſineſs I try'd, ſhe fill'd my mind,
On other Lips my Dear I kis't,
But never ſolid Joy could find
Where I my charming *Silvia* mis't.

# THE
# Banquet of MUSICK:
### O R,
## A Collection of the newest and best SONGS sung at Court, and at Publick Theatres.

### W I T H

## A THOROW-BASS for the *Theorbo-Lute*, *Bass-Viol*, *Harpsichord*, or *Organ*.

*Composed by several of the Best Masters.*

The WORDS by the *Ingenious Wits* of this Age.

## THE FIRST BOOK.

*Gui: Vauahan Sculp:*

LICENSED,
*Nov.* 19. 1687.          *Rob. Midgley.*

*In the SAVOY:*
Printed by E. *Jones,* for *Henry Playford,* at his Shop near the *Temple* Church, 1688.

## JOHN CROWNE

### THE ENGLISH FRIER:
#### OR,
### THE TOWN SPARKS (1689/90)

The main concern of Crowne's play is its satire on the Catholics by means of the character of Father Finical. The story subordinated to this has to do with Lord Wiseman's cast mistress and her covert attempt at revenge by setting Young Ranter to try the virtue of Wiseman's intended wife Laura. In Act V, Scene 2 just before the great moment when Wiseman discovers Ranter in Laura's chamber, she and Airy are alone conversing. Airy has agreed to sing the song that Laura likes, and this is it.

*I once had Virtue, Wealth, and Fame,*
  *Now I'm a ruin'd Sinner,*
*I lost 'em all at Loves sweet game,*
  *Yet think my self a winner.*

*Since that dear Lovely Youth I gain,*
  *My heart was long pursuing,*
*I'm Rich enough, nor shall Complain*
  *Of such a sweet undoing.*

*I'le Laugh at cruell Fortunes spight,*
  *While I have any feature,*
*To keep his Love, for that's delight*
  *Enough for mortall Creature:*

*The Sport's so pleasant, you will own,*
  *When once you have been in it,*
*You'd gladly be an age undone,*
    *For one such Charming-minute.*
                    (1690, Act V, Scene 2)

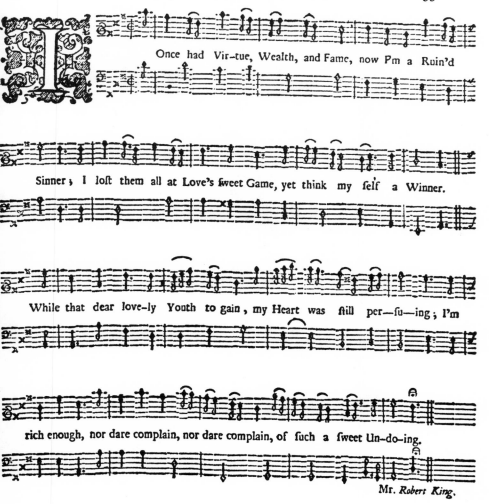

Once had Vir-tue, Wealth, and Fame, now I'm a Ruin'd

Sinner; I loſt them all at Love's ſweet Game, yet think my ſelf a Winner.

While that dear love-ly Youth to gain, my Heart was ſtill per—ſu—ing; I'm

rich enough, nor dare complain, nor dare complain, of ſuch a ſweet Un-do-ing.

Mr. *Robert King.*

## II.

I laugh at cruel Fortune's Spite,
  While I have any Feature,
To keep his Love, for that's delight
  Enough for Mortal Creature:
The Sport's ſo pleaſant, you will own,
  When once you have been in it,
You'd gladly be an Age undone, an Age undone,
  For one ſuch happy Minute.

## THOMAS SOUTHERNE

THE WIVES EXCUSE:
OR,
CUCKOLDS MAKE THEMSELVES (1691)

Mrs. Witwoud has called for a song to divert the company. The dramatist finds it necessary to have her retire long enough to change a scarf by which she intends to personate Mrs. Sightly in the masquerade. The song, performed while she is gone, neatly fills up the hiatus in the action.

Corinna *I excuse thy Face;*
  *The erring Lines which Nature drew:*
*When I reflect, that every Grace*
  *Thy Mind adorns, is just, and true:*
*But oh! thy Witt what God has sent?*
  *Surprizing, airy, unconfin'd:*
*Some wonder sure* Apollo *meant,*
  *And shot himself into thy Mind.*
                    Thomas Cheek (1692, Act V, Scene 3)

O—rin—na, I ex—cuſe thy Face, the er—ring Line which

Na—ture drew; when I re—flect, that ev'—ry Grace thy Mind a—dorns, is

Juſt and True: But Oh! thy Wit what God has ſent, ſur—pri—ſing, ai—ry,

un—con—fin'd; ſome Wonders ſure A—pol—lo meant, and ſhot him—ſelf in-

to thy Mind.                                   Mr. *Henry Purcell.*

## THOMAS D'URFEY

### The Marriage-Hater Match'd (1691/2)

Several of the actors and actresses in D'Urfey's play were brilliant singers as well. He gave them in consequence songs to display their double gifts. Lord Brainless, a "Pert, Noisy, Impertinent Boy . . . a great Admirer of *La Pupsey*, and Jealous of her Lap-dog" went to Bowman who sings this song and one other. Distracted in his courtship by Lady Pupsey's preference for her "Dony," he has composed "*Celadon's* Complaint against Monsieur *Le Chien*." 'Tis writ like a man of quality and he intends to give it to the poet when the next play comes out. Meanwhile he consents to sing it privately to the company.

### The SONG of *Monsieur Le Chien.*

G*Reat* Jove *once made Love like a Bull;*
*With* Læda *a Swan was in vogue,*
*And to persevere in that Rule,*
*He now does descend like a Dog;*
*For when I to* Silvia *would speak,*
*Or on her Breast sigh what I mean;*
*My Heart-strings are ready to break,*
*For there I find* Monsieur Le Chien.

2. *For Knowledge in Modish Intreagues,*
*Or managing well an Amour,*
*I defie any one with two Legs,*
*But here I am Rival'd by four:*
*Distracted all night with my wrongs,*
*I cry, Cruel Gods,—what d'ye mean,*
*That what to my Merit belongs*
*You bestow upon* Monsieur Le Chien.

3 *For Feature or Niceness in Dress,*
*Compare with him surely I can;*
*Nor vainly my self should express,*
*To say I am much more a Man;*
*To the Government firm too, as he,*
*(The former I cunningly mean)*
*And if he Religious can be,*
*I'm as much sure as* Monsieur Le Chien.

4 *But what need I publish my parts,*
*Or idly my Passion relate;*
*Since Fancy that Captivates Hearts*
*Resolves not to alter my Fate:*
*I may Sing, Caper, Ogle, and Speak,*
*And make a long Court* ausi bien,
*And yet with one passionate lick*
*I'm out-rival'd by* Monsieur Le Chien.

(1692, Act III, Scene 2)

Reat *Jove* once made Love like a Bull, a Bull, with *Le—da* a

Swan was in vogue; and to per—fe-vere in that Rule, that Rule, he now does defcend like a Dog:

For when I to *Ce-lia* would fpeak, and on her Breaft figh what I mean; my

Heart-Strings are rea-dy to break, for there I find Monfieur *Le Chien, Le Chien, Le*

*Chien,* Monfieur, Monfieur *Le Chien.*                     Mr. *Montfort.*

## JOHN DRYDEN

### CLEOMENES, THE SPARTAN HERO (1692)

The Ptolomey has fallen into the power of a dangerous siren, Cassandra, who is corrupting him and his kingdom. Dryden opposes the Spartan virtues of his hero, Cleomenes, to her lust. In Act II we are allowed to see her apartment and witness her lascivious methods operating on Ptolomey. This song is part of her paraphernalia of seduction.

*NO no, poor suff'ring Heart no Change endeavour,*
*Choose to sustain the smart, rather than leave her;*
*My ravish'd Eyes behold such Charms about her,*
*I can dye with her, but not live without her.*
*One tender Sigh of hers to see me Languish,*
*Will more than pay the price of my past Anguish:*
*Beware O cruel Fair, how you smile on me,*
*'Twas a kind Look of yours that has undone me.*

2.

*Love has in store for me one happy Minute,*
*And She will end my pain who did begin it;*
*Then no day void of Bliss, or Pleasure leaving,*
*Ages shall slide away without perceiving:*
Cupid *shall guard the Door the more to please us,*
*And keep out Time and Death when they would seize us:*
*Time and Death shall depart, and say in flying,*
*Love has found out a way to Live by Dying.*

(1692, Act II, Scene 3)

N O, no poor suffering heart, no change en—deavour, chuse to suf—

—tain the smart rather than leave her; My ravish'd Eyes behold such Charms a-bout her

I can dye with her, but not live with-out her. One tender sigh of her's

to see me Languish, will more than pay the price of my past Anguish; beware, oh

Cruel, fair how you Smile on me, 'twas a kind look of yours that has undone me.

## II.

Love has in store for me one happy minute,
And she will end my pain who did begin it;
Then no day Void of Bliss, and Pleasure leaving,
Ages shall slide away without perceiving.
*Cupid* shall guard the Door, the more to please us,
And keep out Time, and Death, when they wou'd seize us,
Time and Death shall depart, and say in flying,
Love has found out a way to Live by dying.

The Words by Mr. *Dryden.* Set by Mr. *Purcell.*

## WILLIAM CONGREVE

### THE DOUBLE-DEALER (1693)

Mellefont and Cynthia are two innocents surrounded by a pack of double-dealers eager to spoil the match they have agreed to make. In the end the villains are unmasked. Unwearied nights and wishing days, mutual love, lasting health and circling joys at last attend the pair. In this scene they have been arguing Cynthia's opinion that though marriage "makes man and wife one flesh, it leaves them still two fools; and they become more conspicuous by setting off one another." Fortunately for Mellefont, whose wit lags a little, the musicians cross the stage just then, and he can enforce his arguments by this persuasive song.

### I.

*C*Ynthia *frowns when e're I Woo her,*
   *Yet she's vext if I give over;*
*Much she fears I should undo her,*
*But much more, to lose her Lover:*
*Thus, in doubting, she refuses;*
*And not Winning, thus she loses.*

### II.

*Prithee* Cynthia *look behind you,*
*Age and Wrinckles will o'ertake you;*
*Then too late, desire will find you,*
*When the power does forsake you:*
*Then, O think o'th' sad Condition,*
*To be past, yet wish Fruition.*

           (1694, Act II, Scene 1)

# A Song in the Double-dealler, Sung by Mrs. *Ayliff*,
## Set by Mr. *Henry Purcell.*

Cintbia frowns when e're I Woe her, yet she's vex'd, she's vex'd if I give o—ver;

much, much she fears I shou'd, I shou'd undoe her, but much more, but much more, much

mo———re to lose her Lover; Thus, thus in

doubting she re-fu-fes, and not Winning, and not Winning, thus, thus,

thus she loses; And not Winning, and not Winning, thus, thus, thus, thus,

thus, thus she loses: Prethee *Cintbia* look behind you,

prethee *Cinthia* look behind you, Age and Wrinckles, Age and Wrinckles

will o're--take you; Then, then too late, too late, too late, then, then to late De—

—fire will find you; When the po————————————————w'r does

forfake you;                                        Think, think, oh! think,

think, think,    oh! think, oh! fad con—dition        to be paft,    yet

wifh, yet wifh fru--ition;    to be paft, be    paft,        yet wifh,·

wiſh, wiſh fru—ition, yet wiſh, wiſh, wiſh fru——ition.

## WILLIAM CONGREVE

### LOVE FOR LOVE (1695)

Sailor Ben, "half home-bred and half sea-bred," in spite of his fo'castle manners and speech has taken the fickle heart of Mrs. Frail. To seal their pact he sings her a Song of a Sailor. It was made, he says, "upon one of our Ships-Crew's Wife; our Boat-swain made the Song, may-hap you may know her, Sir [to Scandal]. Before she was Marry'd, she was called Buxom *Joan* of *Deptford*." Scandal admits to having heard her name.

A *Souldier and a Sailor,*
   *A Tinker, and a Tailor,*
*Had once a doubtful strife, Sir,*
*To make a Maid a Wife, Sir,*
      *Whose Name was Buxom* Joan.
*For now the time was ended,*
*When she no more intended,*
*To lick her Lips at Men, Sir,*
*And gnaw the Sheets in vain, Sir,*
      *And lie o' Nights alone.*

2.

*The Souldier Swore like Thunder,*
*He lov'd her more than Plunder;*
*And shew'd her many a Scar, Sir,*
*That he had brought from far, Sir,*
      *With Fighting for her sake.*
*The Tailor thought to please her,*
*With off'ring her his Measure.*
*The Tinker too with Mettle,*
*Said he could mend her Kettle,*
      *And stop up ev'ry leak.*

3.

*But while these three were prating,*
*The Sailor slily waiting,*
*Thought if it came about, Sir,*
*That they should all fall out, Sir:*
      *He then might play his part.*
*And just e'en as he meant, Sir,*
*To Loggerheads they went, Sir,*
*And then he let fly at her,*
*A shot 'twixt wind and water,*
      *That won this Fair Maids Heart.*
                    (1695, Act III, Scene 1)

A soldier and a sai-lor a tinker and a tay-lor, Had

once a doubtful ſtrife Sir, To make a maid a wife Sir, Whoſe

name was buxom Joan, whoſe name was buxom

Joan. And now the time was end-ed, When ſhe no more in-

ten-ded To lick her lips at men Sir and gnaw the ſheets in

vain Sir. And lye o' nights a-lone.

and lye o' nights a-lone.

JOHN ECCLES.

## THOMAS SOUTHERNE

### OROONOKO (1695)

The tone of heroic love and stoic suffering which keeps the action of Southerne's tragedy tense in most of the serious scenes is relieved in Act II by simple merrymaking among the slaves. The songs they listen to are remarkably sophisticated after the Restoration mode, but one must remember that their princely leader Oroonoko had "nothing of Barbarity in his Nature, but in all Points address'd himself, as if his Education had been in some European Court." The stage direction reads: *The Scene drawn shews the Slaves, Men, Women, and Children upon the Ground, some rise and dance, others sing the following Songs.*

### I.

*A Lass there lives upon the Green,*
*Cou'd I her Picture draw;*
*A brighter Nymph was never seen,*
*That looks, and reigns a little Queen,*
*And keeps the Swains in awe.*

### II.

*Her Eyes are* Cupid's *Darts, and Wings,*
*Her Eyebrows are his Bow;*
*Her Silken Hair the Silver Strings,*
*Which sure and swift destruction brings*
*To all the Vale below.*

### III.

*If* Pastorella's *dawning Light*
*Can warm, and wound us so:*
*Her Noon will shine so piercing bright,*
*Each glancing beam will kill outright,*
*And every Swain subdue.*

(1696, Act II, Scene 3)

A Lafs, a Lafs there lives upon the Green, cou'd I, cou'd I, cou'd I her Picture draw; a brighter Nymph, a brigh ter Nymph was never, never, never, never, never feen; that looks and reigns, that looks, and reigns a little, lit--tle, little, lit--tle Queen, a lit--tle, lit--tle, little, little Queen, that kee ps the Swains in awe.

B

Her Eyes are Cupids Darts, and Wings, her

Eyebrows are his Bow, her Silken Hair the Silver Strings, that sure and

swift, swift, swi————ft destruction brings to all, all,

all, to all, all, all, to all, all, all, to all, to all,————

to all the Vale be————low. If *Pastorella's* dawning,

dawning light can warm, and wound, warm and wound, can warm and wound us

fo, her Noon will fhine fo Pier————cing, Peir————cing bright, each

glan————————————cing Beam will kill out————

————right, will kill out-right, and ev——'ry Swain, and ev—'ry Swain fubdue, and

ev——'ry Swain, and ev——'ry Swain fub-—due.

*European Magazine*

RICHARD LEVERIDGE.

From an Original Painting by Fry.

Published by J. Sewell Cornhill. August 1793

# PETER MOTTEUX

## THE ISLAND PRINCESS,
### OR
## THE GENEROUS PORTUGESE (1698/9)

Motteux fends off criticism of his pillage of Fletcher's work, to make his musical play of love and honor in the Spice Islands, with the disarming statement that the original would hardly be relished on the modern stage. "Let this at once satisfie the Modern Critics, and the Zealous Admirers of old Plays; for I neither intended to make it regular, nor to keep in all that I lik'd in the Original, but only what I thought fit for my Purpose, and the success has answer'd my intent, far beyond Expectation." He might have said further in extenuation that the first assaults on Fletcher's work had been made by an anonymous pirate in 1669 and by Tate in 1687. But this admission would have been tantamount to a recognition of the claim of the patentee that Motteux's alterations were not sufficient to allow him the customary author's third day. The only genuinely operatic passage in the adaptation is the incantation scene (Act IV) the music of which moves the King to the cruel act of condemning his sister and her lover to death. For the rest it is chiefly Tate's melodrama eked out with spectacle and musical interludes.

This music, nevertheless, is worthy to be remembered. The example given here is the "ballad" used as the prologue. At the end of the Restoration period an amazing amount of ingenuity was spent in writing prologues which would satisfy the demand for novelty. The height of the fad was reached when "Count" Haynes dressed as an officer of horse delivered his famous epilogue to *Unhappy Kindness* from the back of an ass. For Motteux's opera there were two prologues, one heralding the other and announcing

> since for hum'rous Prologues most you long,
> Before this Play we'll have a Ballad sung.

Enter Mr. *Leveridge*, who sings the following words.

### I.

YOu've been with dull Prologues here banter'd so long,
 *They signifie nothing, or less than a Song.*
*To Sing you a Ballad this time we thought fit;*
*For sound has oft nick'd you, when Sense cou'd not hit.*
  *Then Ladies be kind,*
  *And Gentlemen mind!*

| | |
|---|---|
| *Wit-Carpers,* | *Mobb'd Sinners,* |
| *Play-Sharpers,* | *In Pinners,* |
| *Loud Bullies,* | *Kept-Toppers,* |
| *Tame Cullies,* | *Bench-Hoppers,* |
| *Sowre Grumblers,* | *High-Fliers,* |
| *Wench-Bumblers,* | *Pit-Plyers,* |
| *Give Ear, ev'ry Man!* | *Be still, if you can!* |

*You're always in Mischief for leading the Van.*

2.

*Ye Side-box Gallants, whom the Vulgar call Beaux,*
*Admirers of—Self, and nice Judges of—Cloaths,*
*Who, now the War's over, cross boldly the Main,*
*Yet ne're were at Sieges, unless at* Compiegne.
> *Spare all, on the Stage,*
> *Love in every Age.*

| | |
|---|---|
| *Young Tattles,* | *Young Graces,* |
| *Wild Rattles,* | *Black Faces,* |
| *Fan-Tearers,* | *Some faded,* |
| *Mask-Fleerers,* | *Some jaded,* |
| *Old Coasters,* | *Old Mothers,* |
| *Love Boasters,* | *And Others,* |
| *Who set up for Truth!* | *Who've yet a Colts-Tooth,* |

*See us act that in Winter, you'd all act in youth,*

3.

*Ye Gallery haunters, who Love to Lie Snug,*
*And munch Apples or Cakes while some Neighbour you hug*
*Ye loftier Genteels, who above us all sit,*
*And look down with contempt on the Mob in the Pit!*
> *Here's what you like best,*
> *Jig, Song, and the rest.*

| | |
|---|---|
| *Free Laughers,* | *Sly Spouses* |
| *Close Gaffers,* | *With Blowzes,* |
| *Dry Joakers,* | *Grave Horners,* |
| *Old Soakers,* | *In Corners,* |
| *KindCousins* | *Kind No-Wits,* |
| *By Dozens,* | *Save-Poets,* |
| *Your Custom don't break!* | *Clap till your hands ake;* |

*And though the Wits damn us, we'll say the Whims take.*

(1699, Prologue)

## II.

3/4 Ye Side-Box Gallants, whom the Vulger call Beaus.

Admirers of Self, and nice Judges of Cloaths:

Who now the Wars over, cross boldly the Main,

Yet ne'er were at Sieges, unless at **Campiegne**

Spare all on the Stage, Love in every Age;

3 Young Tattles, Wild Rattles, Fan-Tearers, Mask-Fleerers,

Old Coasters, Lore-Boasters, who set up for Truth:

Young Graces, Black Faces, some Faded, some Jaded,

Old Mothers, and others, who've yet a Colts Tooth:

See us act that in Winter, you'd all act in Youth.

## III.

3/4 You Gallery-Haunters, who love to lye snug,

And maunch Apples or Cakes, while some Neighbour you hugg:

Ye Lofties, Genteels, who above us all sit,

And look down with Contempt, on the Mobb in the Pit.

Here's what you like best, Gigg, Song and the rest;

3 Free Laughers, Close Gaffers, Dry Jokers, Old Soakers:

Kind Cozens, by Dozens, your Customs don't break:

Sly Spousses with Blouses Grave Horners, in Corners;

Kind No-wits, save Poets, clap till your Hands ake,

And tho' the Wits Damm us, we'll say the Whims take.

**For the Flute.**

# THOMAS D'URFEY

## THE FAMOUS HISTORY
### OF
## THE RISE AND FALL OF MASSANIELLO (1699)

The Neapolitan butchers, tailors, millers and cobblers who have helped their fisherman leader Massaniello into the seat of power betray tastes and sentiments that are suspiciously English. This song which opens their feast in Act IV was no doubt intended as a compliment to Massaniello who had glorified his trade by achieving a successful revolution.

O*F all the World's Enjoyments,*
    *That ever valu'd were,*
*There's none of our Employments*
  *with Fishing can compare:*
    *Some Preach, some Write,*
    *Some Swear, some Fight;*
*All Golden Lucre courting,*
  *But Fishing still bears off the Bell,*
*For Profit or for Sporting.*
  Then who a Jolly Fisherman,
    A Fisherman will be,
      His Throat must wet
      Just like his Net,
To keep out Cold at Sea.

### II.

*The Country Squire loves Running*
  *A Pack of well-mouth'd Hounds;*
*Another fancies Gunning*
  *For Wild-Ducks in his Grounds:*
*This Hunts, that Fowls;*
  *This Hawks, Dick Bowls,*
*No greater Pleasure wishing,*
  *But Tom that tells what Sport excells,*
*Gives all the Praise to Fishing.*
  C H O.    Then who, &c.

### III.

*A good* Westfalia Gammon,
  *Is counted dainty Fare;*
*But what is't to a* Salmon
  *Just taken from the* Ware?

*Wheat-Ears and* Quails,
  Cocks, Snipes, *and* Rayles,
*Are priz'd while Season's lasting,*
  *But all must stoop to* Crawfish *Soop,*
*Or I've no Skill in Tasting.*
  C H O.    Then who, &c.

### IV.

*Keen Hunters always take too*
  *Their Prey with too much pains;*
*Nay, often break a Neck too;*
  *A Penance for no Brains:*
    *They Run, they Leap,*
    *Now High, now Deep,*
*Whilst he that Fishing chuses,*
    *With ease may do't,*
    *Nay more, to boot*
*May entertain the Muses.*
  C H O.    Then who, &c.

### V.

*And tho some envious Wranglers,*
  *to jeer us will make bold,*
*And laugh at patient Anglers,*
  *who stand so long i'th' Cold:*
    *They wait on Miss,*
    *We wait on this,*
*And think it easie Labour,*
    *And if you'd know,*
    *Fish profits too,*
*Consult our* Holland *Neighbour.*
  C H O.    Then who a Jolly, &c.

(1700, Act IV, Scene 1)

The Fisherman's SONG in Massaniello Set and Sung by Mr. Leveridge

Of all the Worlds enjoyments, that ever vallu'd were, there's none of our employments, wth Fishing can compare

Some Preach, some Write some Trade, some Fight, all Golden Lucre courting, but Fishing still bears

cho

off the Bell for Profitt or for Sporting. And who a jolly Fisherman, a Fisherman will be; his

Throat must wet, just like his rett, to keep of cold at Sea.

II

The Country Squire loves Runing,
  A Pack of well Mouth'd Hounds;
Another fancyes Guning,
  For Wild ducks in his Grounds;
This Hunts that Fowls,
  That Hawks that Bowls,
No greater Pleasure wishing;
  But he that tells what Sport excells,
Gives all the prize to Fishing,
Cho  And who a jolly &c.

III

A good Westphalia Gamman,
  Is counted dainty fare;
But what ist to a Sammon,
  Iust taken from the ware;
Wheat Ears and Quails,
  Cocks Snipes and Rayls,
Are good whilst Seasons lasting;
  But all must stoop to Craw fish soop,
Or I've no Skill in Tasting.
cho. And who a jolly &c.  For The Flute

IV

Keen Hunters allways take too,
  There Prey with too much Pains.
Nay often break a Neck too.
  A Pennance for no Brains;
They Run they Leap,
  Now high now Deep,
Whilst he that Fishing Chooses;
  At ease may do't nay more to boot.
May entertaint the Muses.
cho  And who a jolly &c.

V

And tho some envious Wranglers,
  To jeer us will make bold;
And laugh at patiant Anglers.
  Who stand so long i'th Cold;
They wait on Miss,
  We wait on this.
And count it easy Labour;
  And if you'd know Fish Profit too,
Consult our Holland Neighbour.
cho. And who a jolly &c.

# GEORGE FARQUHAR

## THE CONSTANT COUPLE;
### OR
## A TRIP TO THE JUBILEE (1699)

That "airy gentleman" Sir Harry Wildair buzzes amorously about Lurewell though his more serious affections, if he can be said to have any, are fixed elsewhere. In this scene he visits her inopportunely as she is engaged in a plot against another of her suitors. He makes his entrance under the pantomime of this song.

*Thus* Damon *knock'd at* Celia's *Door,*
*He sigh'd, and beg'd, and wept, and swore,*
    *The Sign was so,*
      [knocks]
    *She answer'd, No,*
      [knocks thrice]
    *No, no, no,*
*Again he sigh'd, again he pray'd,*
*No,* Damon, *no, I am afraid,*
*Consider,* Damon, *I'm a Maid,*
    *Consider,*
      *No,*
    *I'm a Maid.*
      *No,* &c.
*At last his Sighs and Tears made way,*
*She rose, and softly turn'd the Key,*
*Come in, said she, but do not stay.*
    *I may conclude*
    *You will be rude,*
    *But if you are, you may.*
               (1699, Act IV, Scene 2)

Poor *Damon* knock'd at *Ce‑lia's* door,

Poor *Damon* knock'd at *Ce‑lia's* door;

he sigh'd and beg'd, and wep'd, and‑swore, the sign was so, she an‑swer'd no; the

sign was so, she answar'd no, no, no, no, no: A—gain he

sigh'd, a—gain he pray'd, no, *Damon*, no, no, no, no, no I am a—fraid; con—sider *Damon*

I'm a Maid, con—si‑der *Damon*; no, no, no, no, no, no, no, no I'm a Maid.

At last his Sighs and Tears made way, she rose and softly turn'd the Key;

come in said she, but do not, do not stay; I may conclude, you will be rude, but if you

are you may; I may conclude, you will be rude, but if you will you may.

# NOTES

The notes to the songs are designed to give information, when it can be obtained, on the following points: the writer of the words, in case he is not the dramatist himself; the composer; the singer; the chief seventeenth century appearances of the words and the music; the nature of the rest of the music used in the play. In the instance of the composers, I have emphasized their work for the dramatists, very little of which has hitherto been surveyed. The sources of this information, which limitations of space have prevented me in most cases from indicating, are in general the song books and manuscript collections of theater songs, the single sheet songs and statements in the text of the plays. The only systematic review of a Restoration composer's services to the theater is the late Barclay Squire's "Purcell's Dramatic Music" contributed to the *Sammelbände der internationalen Musikgesellschaft* (1903-1904, pp. 489-564). It is a model guide for anyone venturing into this little-explored territory.

In the notes the date assigned to a play discussed in connection with the work of a theater composer is the year of production.

## The Indian Emperour, p. 13

Pelham Humphrey (1647-1674), nephew, according to Wood, of the noted amateur in music, Colonel John Humphrey, was one of the most gifted of the Children of the Chapel Royal placed under the famous Captain Cooke who had reorganized the singers after the Restoration. At thirteen he received his appointment to the private music as lutenist; four years later his talents as a composer were recognized by a grant (from the Secret Service money) for musical study in France and Italy. He returned in three years with emphatic opinions about the necessity of reforming English music after the new and more dramatic style of Carissimi and Lully, his master in Paris. Pepys, who thought him affected, found him "an absolute Monsieur, as full of form, and confidence, and vanity, and disparages everything, and everybody's skill but his own. The truth is, everybody says he is very able, but to hear how he laughs at all the King's musick here, as Blagrave and others, that cannot keep time nor tune, nor understand anything; and that Grebus, the Frenchman, the King's master of the musick, how he understands nothing, nor can play on any instrument, and so cannot compose: and that he will give him a lift out of his place; and that he and the King are mighty great!" (*Diary*, November 15, 1667, ed. Wheatley, 1896, VII, 184.)

Humphrey did his boasting discretely among friends, for at the time of his early death he was a warden of the corporation of musicians and in great favor at Court as Composer in Ordinary and Master of the Children of the Chapel. Charles II, who made the words for "I pass all my hours in a shady old grove," chose this song of Humphrey's as the best of the compositions performed at the contest of German, Spanish, French and English singers which His Majesty once whimsically commanded fought on the stage in Whitehall (North's *Memoirs of Musick,* ed. Rimbault, 104).

The bulk of Humphrey's music is religious, but the individuality of his secular songs did much to fix the style of the dramatic music of the Restoration. Besides the song given here and the famous "A wife I do hate" from Wycherley's *Love in a Wood* reproduced on p. 19, his theater music includes songs in Dryden's *Conquest of Granada* ("Wherever I am") and Crowne's *Charles VIII* ("O love, if e're thou'lt ease a heart"). His "Where the bee sucks" used in the Shadwell version (1674) as well as the Dryden-Davenant form of *The Tempest* (1667) is preserved in *The Ariel's Songs in the Play call'd the Tempest* (*c.* 1675). Mlle. Pereyra announced in the *Bulletin* of the *Société Française de Musicologie* (October 1920) the discovery, in the Library of the Paris Conservatoire, of his "Song of the Three Devils" and the masque music for the Shadwell version. Humphrey's collaborators in the music for the Shadwell *Tempest* were the most distinguished composers of the moment: Banister, the leader of the King's Band, Locke, Composer in Ordinary to the King, and Battista Draghi, organist to Catherine of Braganza, Charles's consort. Barclay Squire discussed their collaboration in "The Music of Shadwell's Tempest," *Musical Quarterly,* VII, 565-78.

"Ah fading joy" was reprinted without music in *New Court-Songs, and Poems. By R. V. Gent.,* 1672, p. 113 (the text corresponding to the version in the music) ; *Methinks the Poor Town has been troubled too long,* 1673, p. 33; 2nd ed., 1673, p. 50; *The Wits Academy,* 1677, p. 57, Song LXVII.

Humphrey's music was printed in *Choice Ayres, Songs, & Dialogues,* 1675, I, 70 and 1676, I, 66. The scene in the Magician's Cave in Act II of the play requires Kalib to ascend in white in the shape of a woman and sing a prophecy beginning "I look'd and saw within the Book of Fate." No early setting of this exists, but Henry Purcell's music, for the revival in 1691, is preserved in *The Banquet of Musick,* 1692, VI, 14.

### *Juliana, p. 16*

John Banister (1630-1679) was one of that notable group of musicians, including in its circle Pelham Humphrey and Matthew Locke, who did the pleasure of the King by lifting music at the restored Court into a position comparable with that which Lully had given the art under Louis. Banister no doubt received his first lessons from his father who was one of the waits of the parish of St. Giles-in-the-Fields. The son was by 1656 an accomplished violinist, for he appears in the list of the musicians who composed the orchestra playing in D'Avenant's *Siege of Rhodes.*

At the time of Charles's coronation he had already entered the King's employ as violinist. Part of 1662 he spent in France on a substantial pension from the King. The "special service" to which his passport mysteriously refers possibly involved nothing more dangerous than friendly spying on the organization of Louis's famous band of fiddlers, since soon after his return he was commanded by Charles "to make choyce of twelve of our four and twenty violins to be a select band to wayte on us whensoever there should be occasion for musick" (Lafontaine, *The King's Musick,* 159).

Though Banister's future seemed as promising as that of Humphrey, the royal favorite, his prospects began to darken almost immediately. An ominous order was sent to the violins in December 1666 that they and Mr. Banister "doe, from tyme to tyme, obey the directions of Louis Grabu, master of the private musick" (*The King's Musick,* 191). An echo of the rising storm is heard in Pepys's diary. He remarks on February 20, 1666/7, that Banister is "mad that the King hath a French man come to be chief of some part of the King's musique, at which the Duke of York made great mirth." By March Grabu had got his hands on Banister's place. Two reasons can be discerned for the King's disfavor. Wood is sponsor for a story, no doubt a true one, that when Charles once called for the Italian violins, Banister proudly told him he had better have the English (Bodleian MS. Wood D 19[4] f. 14). More serious was his misappropriation of allowances to his band, charged by the players in a petition to Lord Arlington. Banister was, one imagines, only in part guilty. Charles's officers rarely received what on paper was allowed them. He doubtless kept most of the money which passed to him and let the violinists whistle for the rest of the share due them.

Banister continued as a member of the band of royal fiddlers until his death. His virtuosity must still have been appreciated for his salary was exceeded in size by that of only three other royal musicians. Since he was free to engage in private musical ventures, he inaugurated in 1672 the first formal concerts given in England. The advertisement in the *London Gazette* (December 26-30) gave notice "That at Mr. John Banisters House, (now called the Musick-School) over against the George Tavern in White Fryers, this present Monday, will be Musick performed by excellent Masters, beginning precisely at 4 of the clock in the afternoon, and every afternoon for the future, precisely at the same hour."

Roger North left a circumstantial account of these fashionable concerts in his *Musicall Gramarian.* "The first attempt was low; a project of old Banister, who was a good violin, and a theatricall composer. He opened an obscure room In a publik hous In white fryars; filled it with tables & seats and made a side box with curtains for the musick. 1 s a peice, call for what you pleas, pay ye reckoning, & welcome, gentlemen. here came most of the stock performers in towne, and much company to hear; and divers musicall curiositys were presented as, for Instance, Banister himself, upon a flageolett in consort, w$^{ch}$ was never heard before nor since" (ed. H. Andrews, 30-1).

Banister on many happy occasions made music with Pepys and discussed the theory of the art with that eager amateur. He was welcome in a group of donnish musicians at Oxford where on January 11, 1666, Wood heard him perform on his celebrated "little pipe or flagellet in consort; which hath bin about seven years in fashion; but contrary to the rule in musick 30 years [ago] which was grave" (A. Clark, *Life and Times*, 1892, II, 69).

The preponderance of Banister's music is for the theater, and much of it survives. In addition to that printed here from *Juliana* and one from *The Gentleman Dancing Master* on p. 23, the following songs can be found: "Thus all our lives long, we are frolick and gay" (Shadwell's *Royal Shepherdess*, 1669); "Can Luciamira so mistake" (Tuke's *Adventures of Five Hours*, 1663 or later); "The bread is all baked" (D'Avenant's *Man's the Master*, 1668); "Amintas that true hearted swain" (Behn's *Forc'd Marriage*, 1670); "Beneath a myrtle shade" (Dryden's *Conquest of Granada*, 1670).

If Pepys had been of a different mind on one occasion, we might possess Banister's setting to Sedley's lovely "Ah! Cloris, that I now could sit" which was sung by Knipp in *The Mulberry Garden* (1668). He heard the song rehearsed at her lodgings but thought it a "slight, silly short ayre, meanly set" and asked Banister to prick him down the notes to the echo song in *The Tempest*, thus politely covering his distaste for "Ah! Cloris." There is some reason to believe that the Scotch tune "Gilderoy" to which the words of "Ah! Cloris" were sung in the eighteenth century is Banister's air, but the proof is not conclusive, and we must regretfully count the song as lost.

Banister seems to have had a hand in composing the music needed in Catherine Philips's *Pompey* about which she was so anxiously writing her Poliarchus in the winter of 1662/3. She says explicitly, it is true, that Philaster has set two of the songs, Dr. Pett one, "*Le* Grand a *Frenchman,* belonging to the Duchess of Ormond . . . the fourth, and a *Frenchman* of my Lord Orrery's the second . . ." (*Letters from Orinda to Poliarchus*, 1705, p. 120). There exists, however, a manuscript setting of three of these songs with Banister's name attached to the first (Christ Church MS. Music 350). Can he have been the mysterious Philaster? One would like to think this possible, but it is safer to conjecture that for the actual production in Dublin, music of a less amateurish sort was finally procured than that originally provided by Philaster and Dr. Pett and the retainers of the Duchess and my Lord.

About this same time Banister was engaged in composing the music for Stapylton's *Slighted Maid* (1663). We must be particularly sorry that all of it has disappeared, for it was sufficient in amount and varied enough in style to transform the play into a sort of early semi-opera. Banister wrote, according to the notice on the page announcing the cast, the entire "Instrumental, Vocal, and Recitative Musick," a statement which indicates the importance it was to have in the scheme of the play. In view of his predilection for the flageolet referred to above, a stage direction inserted in Act IV after the entrance of Evening and the two Winds is interesting: "Flajolets play afar off."

Banister's share in the two versions of *The Tempest* in 1667 and 1674 was equal to Humphrey's and consists of four songs: "Come unto these yellow sands"; "Dry those eyes"; the echo song "Go thy way" which so delighted Pepys; and "Full fathom five." These were published in *The Ariel's Songs in the Play call'd the Tempest*.[1]

The most ambitious task undertaken by Banister for the stage was the music contributed to Dr. Charles D'Avenant's *Circe* (1677). *Circe* is called a tragedy by its author but it is really a semi-opera demanding instrumental accompaniment to sacrificial scenes, "horrid" music, and songs for furies, dances for the winds and soft symphonies for the movements of the various divinities. Downes, the prompter, remembered that all was well performed and answered the expectation of the company. Three songs from *Circe* exist in print: two in *Choice Ayres and Songs*, 1679, II, "Young Phaon strove" and "Give me my lute"; and one in Banister and Low's *New Ayres and Dialogues,* 1678, "Cease, valiant hero." Six MS. transcripts of the music for the first act, all derived from a common origin, are extant, but the musicologists are agreed that Henry Purcell rather than Banister is the composer. In that case he must have been called on to provide music for a revival when Banister's first act had either been lost or was considered for some reason impossible for further use. The date of this revival is conjecturally set in 1685.

Mrs. Shadwell, the wife of the playwright, played Joanna and sang the song. The parts which she took did not usually require any particular talent as a singer.

The words of the song appeared in *Methinks the Poor Town has been troubled too long*, 1673, p. 10, with slight alterations, and in *The Wits Academy*, 1677, p. 68, Song LXXXII.

---

[1] In advancing the argument (p. 570) in "The Music of Shadwell's Tempest" (see p. 82 above), that this collection contains only the songs used in the 1674 opera, Barclay Squire forgot that Pepys asked Banister for one of them, the echo song, on May 7, 1668.

The music is printed in *Choice Songs and Ayres,* 1673, I, 55 and *Choice Ayres, Songs, & Dialogues,* 1675, I, 52; 1676, I, 52. The two other songs used in the play, a Song of Triumph in Act III and a chorus for Act V, have not come down.

### Love in a Wood, p. 18

For a sketch of Pelham Humphrey, see p. 81.

Mrs. Knipp, a "most excellent, mad-humoured thing" and "pretty enough," to whom Pepys was "Dapper Dicky," played Lady Flippant and sang the song. Every one knows with what ecstasy he taught her "Beauty Retire" and how she filled his ears with wonderful stories of what goes on behind the scenes and allowed him (supreme experience!) to meet and kiss Nelly. Through this fortunate infatuation with his "Barbary Allen," which was not terminated before Mrs. Pepys had good reason to be jealous, we know a great deal about the status and career of this singing actress.

In the present connection the evidence of the *Diary* is principally useful to show how much incidental singing there was in the theater of which the quartos provide no record. Pepys mentions especially Knipp's singing in the *Custom of the Country* (January 2, 1666/7), *The Humorous Lieutenant* (January 23, 1666/7), *The Chances* (February 5, 1666/7), *If You Know Not Me* (August 17, 1667), *The Surprisal* (April 17, 1668), *The Heiress* (February 2, 1668/9).

Though Knipp usually played affected ladies, madcaps and innocent misses, her rôles were important. Her career, which as the *Diary* shows involved many more parts than those that Genest records, ended in 1678. She will appear again in this volume as Lady Fidget and as a priestess of Bellona—a contrast which gives a fair impression of her bizarre repertory.

The words of the song were printed in *Westminster-Drollery,* 1671, p. 5, where they are noted as "The last Song at the Kings House." They appeared also in *Windsor-Drollery,* 1671, p. 10, Song 14; 1672, p. 10, Song 14; and again in *New Court-Songs, and Poems. By R. V. Gent.,* 1672, p. 115, as "A Song in Love in a Wood." The next song following in this last volume is "The Answer" to Lady Flippant's words. It begins:

> A Wife I adore,
> If either shes Constant or Civil:
> But a Pox on a Whore!
> She's Company fit for the Devil:
> On Terms she will stand,
> And will not permit you to enter
> Without Money in Hand,
> But pretend she's unwilling to venture.

*The Wits Academy* which first printed the song in 1677, p. 11, Song XI, carried it through various reprintings into the next century.

The music is found in *Choice Ayres and Songs,* 1684, V, 38. D'Urfey resurrected it for his *Wit and Mirth,* 1712, III, 250. In the musical contest held at Whitehall to satisfy a whim of the King's, this song was performed with Humphrey's "I pass all my hours" as an example of the English proficiency (North, *The Musicall Gramarian,* ed. Andrews, p. 28).

## Marriage A-la-Mode, p. 20

The official record of Robert Smith's service to the King is brief and melancholy. On June 20, 1673, he was admitted musician in ordinary, his instrument being the lute. On August 3, 1674, he was sworn and admitted to the place of Pelham Humphrey deceased. A year and two months later (November 22, 1675) he is dead and Richard Hart has his place (Lafontaine, *The King's Musick,* 255, 274, 295). His early training he had received from Captain Cooke of the Chapel Royal where he was a promising fellow-chorister and student with Blow and Humphrey (*Musical Antiquary,* Vol. II, p. 171).

In the few years of his maturity Smith wrote a prodigious amount of instrumental music, much of which is still in manuscript (Christ Church Library). About the time of his appointment as lutenist to the King the theater took notice of his talent, and for the three remaining years of his life he was much in request at the play-houses. For Shadwell's *The Miser* (1672) he wrote a little country song, "As I walk'd in the woods one evening of late," which is calculated to stir up the girls "more than your Fiddle and Voyces can do," and a catch, "Come lay by your cares, and hang up your sorrow." Dryden employed him to set three songs: "Why should a foolish marriage vow," printed here; "Long betwixt love and fear Phillis tormented" (*The Assignation,* 1672); and "The day is come, I see it rise" (*Amboyna,* 1673). Fiddle's song in praise of country life, "Ah, how I abhor the tumults and smoke of the town," in Shadwell's *Epsom Wells* (1672) was his. Mrs. Behn had two songs from him for *The Dutch Lover:* "Ah false Amyntas," printed on page 25, and "Amyntas led me to a grove." For Arrowsmith's *The Reformation* (1673) he set "Fill round the health" for Tony Leigh to sing in the part of Pacheco. Nevill Payne used his "From friends all inspired" in *The Morning Ramble* (1672) and Ravenscroft had from him "A heart in love's empire" for the *Citizen Turned Gentleman* (1672). The music of all these songs survives.

One brief, intimate glimpse of Smith behind the curtain of time we are allowed. In D'Urfey's *Fool Turn'd Critick* (1676) Betty is asked by Lady Ancient to sing a song set by a very good friend of her kinsman (who made the words)—"one Mr. *Smith*, late composer to the King's Play-House." "Who *Bob*!" replies Timothy, "a very Excellent Fellow Madam, believe me, and one the Town misses very much to my knowledge." Betty sings the song, "I found my Caelia one night undressed." It was, we suppose, his last.

Mrs. Marshall and Mrs. Slade took the parts of Doralice and Beliza and sang their song. Mrs. Marshall was for fifteen years (1663-1677) the principal actress at the King's House. She created many of the great rôles in the heroic tragedies, notably Lyndaraxa (*Conquest of Granada*), Poppea (*Nero*) and Nourmahal (*Aureng-Zebe*). She and Knipp were often cast together as in the pretty scene in the fourth act of *Secret Love* where Knipp as Asteria sang "I feed a flame within, which so torments me" to Marshall as the Queen.

Mrs. Slade is presumably the Betty Slade who acted Lucy in *Love in a Wood* (1671) and sang a French song as Melinda in Fane's *Love in the Dark* (1675).

The words of the song were printed in the year of the play's production (1672) in *New Court-Songs, and Poems. By R. V. Gent.*, 72, where it is headed "A Song at the King's-House."

The music was published in *Choice Songs and Ayres*, 1673, p. 39 and *Choice Ayres, Songs, & Dialogues*, 1675, I, 35 and 1676, I, 35. The song was sung in the next century to another tune given in *The Musical Miscellany*, 1729, II, 52 and *The Merry Musician*, IV, 161. The edition used here is the second, from the *Choice Ayres* of 1675, as the first was so badly offset in printing as to be illegible.

The only other song called for in the play, "Whilst Alexis lay prest," sung in Act IV, Scene 2, was set by Dr. Nicholas Staggins, Master of the King's Music from 1675, when he succeeded Louis Grabu, until his death in 1700. The music is printed in *Choice Songs and Ayres*, 1673, I, 27 and *Choice Ayres, Songs, & Dialogues*, 1675, I, 22 and 1676, I, 22.

### The Gentleman Dancing-Master, p. 22

For a notice of Banister, see p. 82.

The song continued in fashion for thirty years. It was printed immediately after it was first heard in three popular miscellanies: *Windsor-Drollery*, 1672, p. 88, Song 155; *Westminster Drollery, The Second Part*, 1672, p. 1 where it is headed "The late Song at the Dukes House"; *Covent Garden Drolery*, 1672, p. 27. Ebsworth notes that it is also in *Grammatical Drollery*, 1672, but I have not found a copy of this edition. The song was still in request in the early eighteenth century as *The Wits Academy*, which had first printed it in 1677 (p. 40, Song XLVIII), reprints it on p. 188, Song LIV, of the 8th edition (1701). Amusing testimony of the song's vogue turns up in Bourne's unacted *Contented Cuckold* (Q. 1692). The author planned to have Lettice, the maid, sing three songs, at various times, to amuse the company. She was to make a humble remonstrance before commencing: "I'le do my endeavour to please you all if possible, but you know I could never sing well: Besides, I have nothing new to Sing; mine are all old." Her third "old" song was to have been "Since we poor slavish women."

Banister's setting appears in *Choice Songs and Ayres,* 1673, I, 22 and *Choice Ayres, Songs, & Dialogues,* 1675, I, 18 and 1676, I, 18.

### *The Dutch Lover, p. 24*

For an account of Smith, see p. 87.

The words were printed in *London Drollery,* 1673, p. 14, as "The Second Song in the Dutch Lover."

The music of the song was printed in *Choice Songs and Ayres,* 1673, I, 52 and again in *Choice Ayres, Songs, & Dialogues,* 1675, I, 42 and 1676, I, 42.

*The Dutch Lover* requires considerable music. In Act II in a scene (6) suggesting the last sad conversation between Desdemona and Emilia, Cleonte asks Francisca for a song. She sings, to please her own humor, "Amyntas led me to a grove." Smith composed the music for this, and it survives in *Choice Songs and Ayres,* 1673, I, 56. Rural music is needed in Act III and songs for the masque given in Cleonte's honor. Haunce sings a Dutch song in Act IV. It is probable that Smith wrote all the music required in the play, though only these two songs are now to be found.

### *Sophonisba, p. 26*

Henry Purcell (1659-1695) was acknowledged in his own time to have carried off the palm from his associates among the King's musicians. He wore his fame easily. His amiability and love of good living endeared him to the Court, and in the last fifteen years of his life to the dramatists whose plays his music adorned. His genius invites and can withstand comparison with that of his great contemporaries Lully and Bach. Like the latter he was equally distinguished in the secular and the ecclesiastical styles. Similarly there is in everything he wrote richness, vitality and an amazing inventiveness. His work epitomizes the development of English music during the thirty-five years of his life and brings it to a climactic end just before the arrival of new foreign influences with Handel.

Purcell was born into a family of musicians. His father, Composer for the Violins and Master of the Abbey Choristers, died in 1664. His uncle Thomas, an adroit collector of musical posts in Charles's court, undertook the education of young Henry in his craft. The·boy soon learned his uncle's knack of acquiring plural offices. At seventeen he held the important post of copyist at the Abbey. He moved into Matthew Locke's place as Composer in Ordinary for the Violin in 1677. Three years later he became organist at the Abbey on the resignation, in his favor it is said, of his admiring master Dr. John Blow. During these early years the amount of his official writing—anthems for state occasions, welcome odes for royal arrivals and departures, birthdays and other anniversaries—was enormous.

Purcell's connection with the stage began in 1679, if we can rely on the statement of Downes in *Roscius Anglicanus*. The play was Lee's *Theodosius* of which Downes says: "All the Parts in't being perfectly perform'd, with several Entertainments of Singing, compos'd by the famous master Mr. *Henry Purcell* (being the first he ever composed for the stage), made it a living and gainful play to the Company."[1] From 1680 until his death in 1695 Purcell devoted an increasing amount of his energy to the stage, the total of the productions for which he composed music reaching in those fifteen years to fifty-four.

Purcell's talents and sensibility especially fitted him to write dramatic music. No Restoration composer had so nice an ear for the accentuation of English speech. The unconscious training received while he was a music copyist, when hundreds of Elizabethan vocal scores passed under his eyes, gave him a perception in the accommodation of musical phrase to spoken phrase, one of the chief excellencies of Tudor music, which even Dryden was forced to bow to in the *Epistle Dedicatory* to *King Arthur*.

The general run of composers who were employed by the dramatists often worked with little sense of the kind of dramatic expressiveness demanded in a particular scene. Their songs fall easily into the recognized pastoral, convivial, "horror" or "mad-song" categories. Purcell felt the import of the dramatic situation he was required to set and followed with understanding each shift in mood.

This characteristic can be plainly seen in the song given here, even though it was written before the period of his best dramatic work. The priestess is represented by Lee as struggling between two emotions, her longing to escape to the coolness of some silver stream and the irresistible driving fury of the goddess. The music has scarcely begun when the divine afflatus surges into it. An idyllic passage follows; then a section in triple time which marvellously expresses the swelling power of the deity. This bursts finally into the mad and incoherent recitative "O bind me, O bind me about." The concluding

[1] If it can be proved that D'Urfey's *Virtuous Wife* was produced early in the autumn of 1679, which is an allowable assumption in view of the fact that it was announced for publication in the Term Catalogue in November, then Downes's statement may be erroneous since Purcell also wrote music for D'Urfey's play. Mr. Nicoll puts the production of *Theodosius c.* September 1680 which would make certain the priority of *The Virtuous Wife* in the Purcell canon.

passage pictures the gradual weakening and final submission of the priestess.

*Dido and Aeneas,* Purcell's first experiment in opera, was undertaken in 1688 as a favor to his friend, the choreographer Josias Priest, who kept a school for young ladies in Chelsea and needed something by which to display their accomplishments in singing and dancing. At the moment Grabu was the musician generally supposed to be most expert in the mysteries of this kind of composition. Dryden had quite naturally chosen him to set his ill-fated *Albion and Albanius* in 1685. Grabu's magnificent folio edition of the score was in the hands of musicians, and Purcell may have looked on Priest's request as a chance to dislodge the Frenchman.

The artistic triumph of the miniature *Dido and Aeneas* was soon known beyond the group of amateurs who witnessed it. Its immediate effect in Purcell's career was an invitation from the great Betterton to provide the extensive music for the spectacular adaptation of Beaumont and Fletcher's *Prophetess* which he was preparing. The notable advances in operatic style which this work contained led Dryden in turn, after entrusting to him the setting of three songs and the instrumental music for *Amphytrion,* to ask him to collaborate in *King Arthur.* Six years previously Dryden had planned this work as the first genuine English opera to which *Albion and Albanius* was to be a kind of prologue. For the rest of Purcell's life the association between the two men was continuous.

Purcell's masterpiece is undoubtedly the score of *The Fairy Queen,* an extravaganza based on *A Midsummer Night's Dream* but containing so little of Shakespeare's verse that Purcell was not called on to set a single line of the original play. The baroque fancy of the century did not achieve anything more delightful. Fairies, shepherdesses, nymphs and dryads, divinities and seasons, monkeys and human beings mingle in the successive masques in the most amiable and inconsecutive fashion. A Chinese garden, complete with the proper flora and fauna, discloses in the final scene one dazzling marvel after another until its orange trees move to the front of the stage and the whole *revue* ends in a grand dance, a chaconne and a chorus.

The following summary of Purcell's dramatic music is derived from Barclay Squire's detailed article in the *Sammelbände der internationalen Musikgesellschaft,* 1903-1904, pp. 489-564. A few dates of productions given there have been modified to accord with Professor Nicoll's conclusions in his *Restoration Drama.* Plays for which Purcell furnished more than an incidental song or two are here marked with an asterisk.

1679: D'Urfey, *The Virtuous Wife*; Lee, *Theodosius
1681: Tate, *Richard the Second*; D'Urfey, *Sir Barnaby Whig*

?1682: Beaumont and Fletcher, *The Double Marriage* (revival)

?1683: Ravenscroft, *The English Lawyer* (doubtful if the single song was actually used in the play)

1685: C. D'Avenant, *Circe* (revival); Tate, *Cuckolds' Haven*; Lee, *Sophonisba* (revival)

?1686: Beaumont and Fletcher, *Knight of Malta* (revival)

1688: Tate, *Dido and Aeneas*; D'Urfey, *A Fool's Preferment*

1689: Lee, *Massacre of Paris*

1690: Dryden, *Amphytrion*; Betterton, *The Prophetess; or, the History of Dioclesian*; Settle, *Distressed Innocence*; Southerne, *Sir Anthony Love*

1691: Anon., *The Gordian Knot Untied*; Dryden, *The Indian Emperour* (revival); *King Arthur*; Southerne, *The Wives' Excuse*

1692: Dryden, *Aureng-Zebe* (revival near this date), *Cleomenes*; *The Fairy Queen*; Bancroft, *Henry the Second*; Shadwell, *The Libertine* (revival); D'Urfey, *Marriage Hater Matched* (with Mountfort and Tollet); Dryden and Lee, *Oedipus* (revival); Crowne, *Regulus*

1693: Congreve, *Double Dealer*; Shadwell, *Epsom Wells* (revival); Wright, *The Female Virtuosos*; Southerne, *The Maid's Last Prayer*; Congreve, *The Old Bachelor*; D'Urfey, *Richmond Heiress* (with Eccles); Beaumont and Fletcher, *Rule a Wife and Have a Wife* (revival)

1694: Ravenscroft, *Canterbury Guests*; D'Urfey, *Don Quixote*, Part I (with Eccles) and Part II (with Eccles and Pack); Southerne, *Fatal Marriage*; Dryden, *Love Triumphant* (with Eccles); Crowne, *Married Beau* (with Eccles); Dryden, *Spanish Friar* (revival); Shadwell, *Timon of Athens* (revival)

1695: Behn, *Abdelazar* (revival); *Bonduca* (anonymous alteration of Beaumont and Fletcher's play); D'Urfey, *Don Quixote*, Part III (with Courteville, Morgan and Akeroyde); Dryden, *Indian Queen* (an operatic adaptation completed by Daniel Purcell); Scott, *Mock Marriage*; Southerne, *Oroonoko*; Gould, *Rival Sisters*; Shakespeare-Dryden-D'Avenant-Shadwell, *The Tempest* (revival); Dryden, *Tyrannick Love* (revival)

1696: Norton, *Pausanias* (with Daniel Purcell)

The Purcell Society has issued all his dramatic and operatic music in the following volumes of *The Works of Henry Purcell*, 1878-  : II (The Masque in *Timon*); III (*Dido and Aeneas*); IX (*Dioclesian*); XII (*The Fairy Queen*); XVI, XX, XXI (Dramatic Music); XIX (*The Indian Queen* and *The Tempest*); XXVI (*King Arthur*).

For an analysis of the operas and more important songs, see E. J. Dent, *Foundations of English Opera,* Chapters IX-XI.

In the 1685 quarto and in later editions of *Sophonisba* the parts of Aglave and Cumana are entered as performed by Mrs. Nep and Mrs. Corey respectively. The latter undoubtedly continued in the rôle until the time of her retirement in 1692. She must, then, have sung the mad song in its original setting and possibly in Purcell's version, when that was, as is assumed below, composed for a revival.

Mrs. Corey, so Downes declares, came into the King's Company in 1663, where she divided with Mrs. Gwynn, Mrs. Marshall and Mrs. Knipp the principal female rôles in the repertory. She created, among others, the parts of the Widow Blackacre (*Plain Dealer*), Octavia (*All for Love*) and Lady Fantast (*Bury Fair*). Her voice was an asset to her acting even when her age compelled her to play shrews and ancient serving women. As late as 1690 in Mountfort's *Successful Strangers,* a play which was enlivened with a good deal of singing, she sang a dialogue with the popular and gifted Bowen.

Purcell's music is in *Orpheus Britannicus,* 1702, II, 47. It has been asserted (article on Lee in the *D.N.B.*) that this song was the first music composed by Purcell for the stage. Barclay Squire proposed with reason that it was more certainly sung in a revival in 1685 or 1693 (*op. cit.,* 549). The use of considerable incidental music beside this song is suggested in the text. In Act I, Scene 2, King Massinissa is discovered in a pleasant grotto to the sound of soft music. A lofty march for trumpets makes a ceremony of his entrance after the victory over Syphax (Act III, Scene 2). Cumana sings a prophecy of war after the mad song, and the spirits who dance in this temple scene must have been provided with something to dance to.

### Gloriana, p. 28

The music was printed in *Choice Ayres and Songs,* 1679, II, 26 with no mention of the composer. The rest of the vocal music in the play can be found. The rousing song with which the curtain lifts, "Let business no longer usurp your high mind," came from the hand of Dr. Staggins. It is given in *Choice Ayres and Songs,* 1684, V, 42. "How severe is fate to break a heart," sung in Act V before the wronged Caesario rises *solus* "as from Sleep," is also the work of Staggins. It is printed in *Choice Ayres and Songs,* 1679, II, 47.

### A Fond Husband, p. 31

William Turner (1651-1740), whose father was a cook at Pembroke College, Oxford, learned to sing in the choir in Christ Church. His proficiency soon got him a place in the Chapel Royal under Captain Cooke. When his voice changed into a magnificent counter-tenor, he remained in the Chapel as one of the gentlemen. In 1672 he became musician in ordinary, for both lute and voice, in the private music. He continued to receive the favor of the Court under James and William (Lafontaine, *The King's Musick, passim*).

Meanwhile Turner worked seriously at composition, and his reputation as a composer grew until some presumed to mention him as a rival to Purcell. He proceeded Mus.D. at Cambridge in 1696. An anonymous admirer who celebrated this honor in elegant Latin verses spoke of him, somewhat ambiguously, as

> . . . PURCELLO indoctior uno
> Cantor TURNERUS, cui Musica dextera suaves
> Designat modulos. . . .

The King occasionally lent Turner to the royal theaters. In May 1674, by command, he was allowed to remain in town all week to perform in the operatic *Tempest,* returning to Windsor only for the Sunday services (*op. cit.,* p. 271). Later in the same year (February 1674/5) he sang a principal rôle in Crowne's masque of *Calisto* over which the Court was for weeks in a ferment of preparation (*op. cit.,* 280). His reputation as a teacher of singing was considerable.

In spite of his association with the theater and his convivial nature, which inspired scores of vigorous catches, Turner composed little for the stage. Aside from this song from *A Fond Husband,* there can now be found three songs from Shadwell's *Libertine* (1675): "Thou joy of all hearts"; "Cloris when you dispense your influence"; and the "Song of Devils" in Act V (this last in B.M. Add. MS. 22,100, f. 103). A setting for "Beneath a shady willow" from D'Urfey's *Madam Fickle* (1676) is in B.M. Add. MSS. 19,759, f. 10 and 33,234, f. 34.

Some of Dr. Turner's biographers attempt to thrust on him the theater songs of a later contemporary, a dull fellow who unfortunately bears the same name. As the learned Doctor always appears with his title in the song books, there is no necessity for this confusion.

The song was printed in *Wit and Drollery,* 1682, p. 312 under the title "Silvander Advis'd," in *A New Collection of Songs and Poems. By Thomas D'Urfey, Gent.,* 1683, p. 31, and in *Wits Cabinet,* 1703, p. 139, with the title "In Praise of Marriage." The music survives in *Choice Ayres and Songs,* 1679, II, 30.

The play required five songs, two of which were sung by the versatile Betty (Mrs. Napper). "In January last on Munnoday at morn," with which she obliged the company in Act I, was printed in *Choice Ayres and Songs,* 1679, II, 46. Otway borrowed this in the next year for his *Friendship in Fashion.*[1] Fumble's ballad "And he took her by

---

[1] The melody was subsequently used for many songs. It appears as "The Bony brow" in a collection of Scottish melodies known as the Leyden MS. (*c.* 1695). When Scott appropriated the tune for his "Jock o' Hazeldean" in 1816 (*Albyn's Anthology,* 1816, I) it was generally known as "Willie and Annet." See A. Moffat, *Minstrelsy of Scotland,* 1895, p. 270.

the middle small" (Act V) was a favorite in the Restoration. It is also sung in Act IV of Rhodes's *Flora's Vagaries* (1663) and Powell's *A Very Good Wife* (1693). The music for "The joys of a lover," sung by Rashly in Act I, and "In vain, cruel nymph," sung by Betty in the same act, would appear to be lost.

### *Brutus of Alba, p. 34*

Three "Mr. Wrights" of the day were sufficiently interested in the theater to make it possible to assign the authorship of this song to any one of them. The likeliest candidate is James Wright, antiquarian and amateur poet, the author of *Country Conversations* (1694), which discusses the decline of contemporary comedy into insipidity, and of the brief but most useful *Historia Histrionica* (1699). "J. Wright, Esq." wrote for Mrs. Behn the words of "Fair nymph, remember all your scorn," sung in *The Young King* (1679).

Thomas Farmer (d. 1688) is another of the royal musicians who possessed extraordinary talents in composition in addition to their skill as performers. Wood states (Bodleian MS. Wood D 19[4] f. 51) that he "was of a company of musitians in London, and play'd in the Waytes." By 1671 he was in the King's service as violinist, receiving in 1675 a permanent post as musician in ordinary. Four years later, November 6, 1679, the place of John Banister in the private music, vacant by his early death, was given Farmer (Lafontaine, *The King's Musick,* 342). Cambridge made him a Mus.B. in 1684.

In the reign of James he performed both as a counter-tenor and violinist. His death can be closely dated by a brief note on December 8, 1688, in the Lord Chamberlain's accounts: "John Abraham appointed bowmaster in the place of Thomas Farmer, deceased" (*op. cit.,* 390).

Nahum Tate and Henry Purcell combined to mourn his death in an Elegy published in *Orpheus Britannicus* (1702, II, 35).

> What can [they ask] the drooping Sons of Art,
> From this sad Hour impart,
> To charm the Cares of Life,
> And ease the Lover's Smart.

Farmer composed music for at least eleven plays. Besides this song from *Brutus of Alba,* settings for the following can be traced: "Let's drink, dear friends" (Ravenscroft's *Citizen Turned Gentleman,* 1672); "Come Jug, my honey" (Otway's *Cheats of Scapin,* 1676); "Sitting by yon river side" (Behn's *Sir Patient Fancy,* 1678); "Can life be a blessing" (Dryden's *Troilus and Cressida,* 1679); "Let the traitors plot on" (D'Urfey's *Virtuous Wife,* 1679); "Blush not redder than the morning" (Lee, *Caesar Borgia,* 1680);

"Bonny lass gin thou wert mine" (Otway's *Soldier's Fortune*, 1680) ;
"Phillis, whose heart was unconfined" (Behn's *The Rover*, II, 1680) ;
"Wake, oh Constantine" (Lee's *Constantine*, 1683). Instrumental
music by Farmer for Lee's *Princess of Cleves* (1681) is preserved
in B.M. Add. MSS. 29,283-5 ; I, f. 62b ; II, 61b ; III, 68b.

The music to this song is found in *Choice Ayres and Songs,* 1681,
III, 2.

The play required music for a dance of masquers, a horror tune, a
song for a priestess and attendants and a charm (probably in recitative) for Ragusa. None of these survives.

In 1696 Powell's opera *Brutus of Alba, or Augusta's Triumph* was
produced at Dorset Garden. It pursues the story of Brutus in England
but is not, as some authorities state, an adaptation of Tate's play. Daniel
Purcell supplied the music which he published under the title *The
Single Songs, With the Dialogue, Sung in the New Opera, Call'd
Brutus of Alba,* 1696.

### The Virtuous Wife, p. 36

No song of the period was so much sung and parodied as "Sawney."
Its words could easily be adapted to all sorts of domestic and political
situations, and its insistent tune was immediately fitted to a number
of ballads. The original words are found in *Wit and Drollery,* 1682,
p. 321 under the title "Sawnies Neglect." They show a pointed alteration, in the first stanza, from the version in the play.

> I gave him a fine *Scotch* Sark and Band,
> I gave him a House, and I gave him Land,
> I let him angle in my Fish-Pond,
> But *Sawney* will nere be my Love again.

D'Urfey printed the words in his *A New Collection of Songs and
Poems,* 1683, p. 39. For other early appearances of the text, see Day,
*Songs of Thomas D'Urfey,* 147. Sawney's knavery was rebuked in
"Jennie's Answer to Sawney ; Wherein Love's Cruelty is requited ; or,
The Inconstant Lover justly Despised" (*Roxburghe Ballads,* ed. J. W.
Ebsworth, VII, 15).

In Ravenscroft's *London Cuckolds* (1681) the linkboy sings
"Sawney" as he is "going along" in Act III. An ironic reflection of the
ballad's vogue occurs in Mrs. Behn's *Emperor of the Moon* (1687).
Mr. Jevern [i.e., Jevon] who speaks the prologue has been blaming
the "dull ungrateful Age" for its indifference to the dramatists who
try to please it with themes of love and honor. In desperation they
have now bought a share in the speaking head which forthwith

> *rises upon a twisted
> Post, on a Bench from under the Stage. After* Jevern *speaks to
> its Mouth.*

Oh!—Oh!—Oh!
Stentor Oh!—Oh!—Oh!
*After this it sings* Sawney, *Laughs, crys God bless the King in order.*

The first of the "Sawney" parodies, a broadside attack on the Earl of Danby, is called "The Disloyal Favourite or, The Unfortunate States-Man." It is found among the Roxburghe Ballads (ed. Ebsworth, IV, 80). As Ebsworth remarks, the parallel between Danby's treachery and fall and false Sawney's wickedness is shrewdly carried out. The Danby party answered immediately with "The Loyal Feast," which begins "Tony was small, but of noble race." The Tony is, of course, Anthony Cooper, Earl of Shaftesbury. This is in the Roxburghe collection (V, 148). It is printed also in *A Choice Collection of 180 Loyal Songs,* 1685, p. 195.

"The Loyal Feast" was at once capped with an "Answer to the Pamphlet called 'The Loyal Feast' or, A True Description of his Majestie's deep-dy'd Protestants: the true-begotten Sons of the Whore of Babylon" (*Roxburghe Ballads,* VIII, Part II, 755). The first line reads: "Tories are fools of the Irish race." There is also a marked imitation of the form of the ballad in "The Unfortunate Whigs" (*Roxburghe Ballads,* V, 140):

> The Whigs are but small, and of no good Race,
>     and are belov'd of very few;
> Old Tony broach'd his Tap in ev'ry place,
>     to encourage all his Factious Crew.

This was sung, however, to the tune "The King enjoys his own again."

With the one exception, just noted, all these ballads were sung to the Sawney tune. This was first published in *Choice Ayres and Songs,* 1681, III, 9. It appears with great frequency during the next twenty years. Henry Playford's popular collection of dance tunes, *Apollo's Banquet,* which was worn to pieces in so many pockets that it is now extremely rare, prints it as No. 27 in the edition of 1690 (the 6th), the only copy of the work which I have been able to see. In J. Playford's *Dancing Master* it is on p. 96 in the 9th edition (1695). It was transformed into an instrumental lesson in the second edition of *Musick's Recreation on the Viol, Lyra-way,* 1682. D'Urfey gives it in *Wit and Mirth,* 1699, p. 133 and in later expanded editions of this collection—*Wit and Mirth,* 1707, 1714, I, 133 and 1719, I, 316.

At least seven ballads of the day made use of the tune. The satire on Tony is followed in the *Loyal Songs* (p. 197) by a bawdy poem on Titus Oates, the informer: "The Sodomite or the Venison Doctor, with his brace of Aldermen-Stags," sung to the tune of "Sawney." The Roxburghe Ballads yield "The Poet's Dream: or, The Great Out-cry and Lamentable Complaint of the Land against Bayliffs and their Dogs"

(VII, 11). In the same collection is "The Scornful Maid and the Constant Young-Man" (IX, 867). This could also be sung to the tunes "Times' Changeling" and "A fig for France." The Pepys Ballads supply two other instances of the tune's use: "The poor Peoples Complaint of the Unconscionable Brokers and Talley-Men" (sung also to "This is the cause that the Land complains") and "A King and No King: Or, King James's Wish." The first of these is printed in *The Pepys Ballads*, ed. H. D. Rollins, III, 87; the second in IV, 165 of the same collection. In the *Bibliotheca Lindesiana* two more ballads to "Sawney" can be found: "The Credulous Virgins complaint, Or, lovers made Happy at last. Being a Caution to the Female Sex. Being a most pleasant new Song in two parts, With the Youngmans kind Answer" (No. 246) and "Poor Robins wonderful Vision: Or Englands Warning-piece. Being many strange and miraculous Observations, the like not known in any Age" (No. 1291).

In the eighteenth century the ballad "Corn Riggs are Bonny" was sung to "Sawney." The earliest instance of this connection I find is a single sheet engraving in the British Museum—G. 310 (86). (No. 126 in this collection—"Corn Riggs are Bonny Sung by Miss Jameson at Vauxhall"—is adapted to an entirely different tune.) Chappell (*Popular Music of the Olden Time*, II, 619) states that "it is nowhere called *Corn riggs are bonny*, until after the publication of Allan Ramsay's song commencing, 'My Patie is a lover gay,' in the *Tea Table Miscellany*." From its typography I believe, however, that the single-sheet is earlier.

Chappell suggested (*op. cit.*, 618) that Farmer composed the Sawney tune.

Most of the music used in the play still exists. In Act I Mr. Crotchet [Bowman], the singing-master, offers to sing for Sir Frolic a merry song, "though 'tis not customary with us Professors." His contribution, "Let the traitors plot on" (set by Thomas Farmer) was published in *Choice Ayres and Songs*, 1681, III, 7. Sir Lubberly Widgeon [Tony Lee] sings in this act a ballad on Slow Will of Stenson and pretty Pegg of Benson. This is the well known "Opportunity Lost, or the Scotch Lover Defeated" (*Bibliotheca Lindesiana*, No. 1132). In Act IV he sings a snatch of "For he that a bonny brisk widow will wed." This I have not been able to identify.

Henry Purcell apparently wrote the original instrumental music for the play, possibly as his first service to the theater (see p. 90). The overture and seven of the act-tunes were printed in *A Collection of Ayres, Compos'd for the Theatre*, 1697. The eighth is found in MS. in the Royal College of Music.

Another set of act-tunes for the play is copied as "The Tunes in ye Vertuous Wife . . . Mr. [Jeremiah] Clarke" in B.M. Add. MS. 35,043, ff. 38 and 39. The manuscript, which contains a vast quantity of theater music of the last quarter of the seventeenth century, has been dated 1694-1697. If the conjectured date of Clarke's birth, 1669 (*D.N.B.*), is anywhere near the right year, these tunes would have been composed when Clarke was a boy or a very young man. It is most likely to suppose that they were written for a revival early in the '90's.

### The Orphan, p. 38

Francis Forcer ( ?1650-?1705), though well known as a musician during the Restoration period, wrote little for the theater. In 1697, with James Miles as his partner, he leased the establishment of Sadler's Wells, already popular as a resort for recreation. Their Music House speedily became the best place in London to hear the latest music from the Court and the theaters. Because of his friendship with the song writers Forcer could satisfy his patrons with more modish music than was provided by Britton, the small-coals man in Clerkenwell, or Hubert who combined the exhibition of stuffed animals and other natural curiosities with music-making at the Mitre near St. Paul's.

Besides this song from *The Orphan* the only theater music by Forcer which appears to exist is a setting for "How wretched is the slave to Love" sung in Shadwell's *Virtuoso* (1676).

The music for "Come all ye youths" was published, as given here, in *Choice Ayres and Songs*, 1681, III, 24. *Wit and Mirth* (1700, II, 251) gives the melody only. At least three other musical settings were current in the next century. One is found in B.M. G 307 (113) with the title "The Power of Beauty." The flute arrangement at the bottom of the sheet is signed P.H. Another arrangement ("Castalio's Complaint") was published in *The Musical Miscellany*, 1729, I, 50, without the composer's name. Dr. Boyce's setting must have been widely known for it was issued at least three times: in *The British Musical Miscellany*, II, 125; *Calliope or English Harmony* (*c*. 1738), I, 76; *The London Magazine*, April 1752, p. 185.

The quarto does not suggest the use of any other incidental vocal music in the original production.

### The Disappointment, p. 41

Southerne depended on his friends to supply him with lyrics for his plays. He was indebted for such a service to Etherege and Colonel Sackville in the instance of *The Disappointment*. In other plays of his we find songs by Sackville, Thomas Cheek, Anthony Henley, Congreve, D'Urfey and various "unknown hands" and unidentified poetical "ladies."

Etherege, it will be observed, wrote the words to the next song in this collection.

Captain Simon Pack (not Henry as the article in Grove's *Dictionary* calls him) was for a few weeks a national hero. The episode in military history which made his name familiar to everyone in the kingdom has escaped the musical biographers. They have assumed that the score of songs to which his name is attached in the music books entitle him to a notice as only an obscure hack composer of the day who was occasionally employed by the dramatists when they needed a tune. Pack wrote music as an avocation; his real business was writing ironic letters to his superior, the Secretary of War, and braving King James to the point of treason.

In *Choice Ayres and Songs,* 1679, II, where he first bows as a composer, Pack is Mr. Simon Pack, Gent. He was, as a matter of fact, already a captain, as his first commission—in Sir Henry Goodrick's Regiment of Foot—is dated February 26, 1678 (C. Dalton, *English Army Lists, 1661-1714,* I, 219). Pack saw service in Flanders in that year.

Goodrick's regiment was disbanded in March 1679. Pack's next commission, in the Princess Anne of Denmark's Regiment of Foot, is dated June 19, 1685 (Dalton, II, 29). On the same date a commission as ensign in the same regiment was granted to Thomas Southerne. (Was it chance or design that brought the companions of the playhouse together under the same command?) Since James's natural son, the Duke of Berwick, commanded the regiment, the King surveyed its activities carefully. His personal interest led him to make with it the disastrous experiment of recruiting Irishmen into the army, which caused the famous "revolt of the Portsmouth captains"—one of whom was Pack. The disturbance, which the whole nation watched with excitement, is succinctly described by Bishop Burnet:

They [the captains] said, they had raised their men upon the duke of Monmouth's invasion, by which their zeal for the king's service did evidently appear. If the king would order any recruits, they doubted not, but that they should be able to make them. But they found, it would give such an universal discontent, if they should receive the Irish among them, that it would put them out of a capacity of serving the king any more. But as the order was positive, so the duke of Berwick was sent down to see it obeyed. Upon which they desired leave to lay down their commissions. The king was provoked by this to such a degree that he could not govern his passion. The officers were put in arrest, and brought before a council of war [September 10, 1688], where they were broken with reproach, and declared incapable to serve the king any more (*History of My Own Time,* 1833, III, 284).

Burnet says nothing of the fact that James, in fear of public resentment, commuted the sentence of death, concurred in by Lord Churchill (later the Duke of Marlborough), to dismissal and repaid the captains the cost of their commissions and their expenses incurred in raising their companies (*Hist. Records of the King's Liverpool Regiment,* pp. 6-8).

In December 1688 Pack was made a captain in Colonel Solomon Richard's Regiment of Foot (Dalton, II, 257), but he evidently stayed in this command for only a few months. On April 1, 1689, he wrote to the Secretary of War from Coventry to inform him that he is preparing to march to Carlisle as ordered, though the King had given him leave, because of his recent severe illness, to continue in London (B.M. Add. MS. 38,695, f. 152). The regiment with which he is connected is his old one, the Princess Anne, now the loyal soldiers of King William.

Another letter of Pack's in the same manuscript (f. 154) pictures the desperate need of the regiment for arms and clothing as well as new recruits. Pack delicately phrases the situation to the Secretary: "I . . . march'd away as good a Regiment in all respects as ever I saw uncloath'd." His promotion to Colonel came early in 1689, as a reward, one supposes, for the valor and astuteness which he showed in this difficult northern campaign. Pack disappears from the records of his regiment by 1702 after having served with it at the Boyne and the second siege of Limerick (Dalton, III, 107).

One further item from his military record arrests our attention because we have a clue to its significance which the military historians lack. William reviewed his regiments at Dundalk camp late in October 1689. The comment on the condition of the troops of the Princess Anne reads: "Major very assiduous, but the Lt.-Col. neglects the Regiment" (C. Walton, *History of the British Standing Army,* 1894, p. 80). We know, if the King did not, what Pack was doing when he should have been inspecting buttons and arranging billets.

In the extremely busy years between 1680 and 1694 Pack composed music for at least eight plays. He gave Dryden a setting for "Farewell, ungrateful traitor" (*Spanish Friar,* 1680). Mrs. Behn had music from him for "A pox upon this needless scorn" (*The Rover,* II, 1680) and "How strangely does my passion grow" (*The False Count,* 1682). His other settings include a serenade, "The larks awake the drowsy morn," sung in *The Injured Princess* (D'Urfey, 1682); "Welcome mortal to this place" (Otway, *The Atheist,* 1683); "Tell me Thyrsis, tell your anguish" (Dryden and Lee's *Duke of Guise,* 1683); "Damon let a friend advise ye" (D'Urfey's *Don Quixote,* II, 1694).

Pack was best known, as a composer, for his song "Would you be a man in fashion," published first in *Choice Ayres and Songs,* 1684, V, 14 and parodied subsequently many times in anti-popish ballads.

Since Wiltshire, who played the part of Alberto, sang other songs in the play, it is probable to suppose that he performed this one, though the text does not state that the actor was the singer. Wiltshire's career can be followed from 1677 to 1685, but he does not appear to have performed singing rôles in any other plays.

Captain Pack's setting of "See how fair Corinna lies" is in *The Theater of Music,* 1685, I, 2.

Three other songs were sung in the first production. The play opens with "I never saw a face till now," sung apparently by Alberto while he is dressing. It was set by Pack and printed in *The Theater of Music,* 1685, I, 1. A melancholy song to fit Erminia's despairing mood is sung in her chamber (Act II, Scene 1). The music for "Poor, ill-instructed, wretched woman-kind" is not discoverable. In Act III, Scene 1 "O why did e'er my thoughts aspire" serves as a prelude to Alberto's assignation. Robert King's music for it is found in *The Theater of Music,* 1685, I, 4.

Louis Grabu's instrumental music, eleven tunes used between the acts, exists in a manuscript arrangement for string trio in B.M. Add. MSS. 29,283-5; I, II, f. 74b; III, f. 70b. It is definitely headed in the first volume: "Grabos for Ye Play call'd ye Disappointment, or ye Mother in fashion 1684."

### *A Duke and No Duke, p. 44*

Signior Giovanni Battista Draghi came to England early in the reign of Charles II. Husk conjectured (article in Grove) that he was the brother of Antonio Draghi, Kapellmeister to the Court of Vienna. Pepys met him on that famous occasion at Lord Brouncker's (February 12, 1666/7) when he discussed the possibility of Italian opera in England with Tom Killigrew. Of Draghi he says: "He himself is the poet as well as the musician; which is very much, and did sing the whole [an act from an opera composed by him] from the words without any musique prickt, and played all along upon a harpiscon most admirably, and the composition excellent. The words I did not understand, and so know not how they are fitted, but believe very well, and all in recitativo very fine" (*Diary,* ed. Wheatley, 1895, VI, 162). Draghi's harpsichord playing was considered as marvellous as the performance on the violin of another foreigner, Baltzar the Lübecker, who confounded all the music masters in Oxford.

Signior Draghi was principal organist in the royal Catholic Chapel in Somerset House where he supplanted Locke, though he, we are gratified to know, was still allowed "a chamber organ yt stood by, wch he accompanied with. so just are Kings & queens sometimes" (North, *Musicall Gramarian,* ed. Andrews, 30). In 1680 Draghi was in some danger of being sent out of the kingdom with three other foreign musicians because of his religion. They petitioned on November 16 for the speedy payment of their wages, "being four years in arrears" (Cal. S.P. Dom. 1679-1680, p. 284). Charles, with his usual wit, had supported Draghi with bounty from funds of the secret service (Camden Soc., Vol. 52, *Moneys . . . for Secret Services,* 93).

Draghi's first work for the theater was a part of the instrumental music in Shadwell's *Psyche* (1674/5) to which Evelyn possibly refers as "an Italian opera . . . the first that had ben in England of this kind" (*Diary*, ed. Wheatley, 1879, II, 299). Locke composed the songs and published them with his instrumental music for the opera in *The English Opera; or, the Vocal Musick in Psyche*, 1675. Draghi's music was never printed nor were his dance tunes for Shadwell's *Tempest* given in 1674. Two songs in *A Duke and No Duke* were composed in 1685. To Mountfort's *Injur'd Lovers* (1687/8) he contributed "Lucinda close or veil those eyes." In Harris's *The City Bride* (1696) the dialogue "A woman's love and man's is such" is headed "set by Seignior Baptist."

The similarity of Draghi's name to that of the Gallicized Italian, Lully, has often betrayed his biographers. I suspect that this confusion has been responsible for the assertion that Draghi wrote music for D'Urfey's *Wonders in the Sun* since I can find no warrant for this statement. In Act III (1706, p. 53) a note in the text declares, however: "This Dialogue is made to a Famous Sebel, of Seignour Baptist Lully."

The only music actually performed in the play helps Spirits to "rise and dance about Lavinio, who by a Device is transform'd before the Audience into his own appearance, and Habit" (Act V). It does not survive. The three songs sung between the acts, of which this is the first, were printed, with their music, at the end of the play. The second is Robert King's "Ah poor Olinda!" and the third Draghi's "Who can resist my Celia's charms?" When Tate's farce was completely altered by Robert Drury into a ballad opera, *The Devil of a Duke*, in 1732, the twenty-one songs which were introduced did not include any of these used in the original production. But the original songs had perhaps been discarded before that. In D'Urfey's *Wit and Mirth*, 1707, IV, 112 there is printed "*A New* Song *in the Play call'd*, (A Duke and no Duke,) *Sung by Mrs.* Cibber," the first line of which is "Damon if you will believe me." Another song, used in a revival about 1692, was composed by Raphael Courteville (see p. 119).

### Cuckolds-Haven, p. 46

For Purcell, see p. 89.

This song is an excellent specimen of the topical music which invaded the drama with increasing frequency toward the end of the century. There is a large amount of such music in the song books, loosely identified as "A New Song at the Theater" or "The Latest New Song at the Playhouse." This particular one is printed in *The Second Book of the Pleasant Musical Companion . . . The Second Edition*, 1686, Part III, No. 10. The alphabetical table states that it is a "new song." A MS. copy exists in the Fitzwilliam Museum (No. 120). It escaped the notice of Barclay Squire in his list of Purcell's theater music, but was printed by him in the Purcell Society's edition of the *Works*, XXII, 43 (*Catches, Rounds, Two-part and Three-part Songs*).

Very little music was sung in the play itself, and none of it survives. The affected Girtred hears "the French song"—"The wise believe that I love none"—in Act I, Scene 3 and Security, to justify his boast that he can make ten times better music than one hears at the "Musick-House in the Fields," sings "The Froe She wan an Excise, &c" (Act II, Scene 2).

### *Bellamira, p. 48*

Shadwell's connection with *Bellamira* extended to more than the present to Sedley of this setting of "Thyrsis unjustly you complain." In the "Preface to the Reader" of the quarto Sedley states that a friend came to his chamber as he was at work on the first act. He offered to give this friend the play to present under his own or another's name. This could not, it seems, be arranged, but Sedley produced the play himself and gave this mysterious friend the proceeds of the author's benefit on the third night. As Mr. De Sola Pinto suggests (*Sir Charles Sedley*, 1927, p. 168) the "friend" was probably Shadwell, who according to Oldys owed whole scenes to Sedley and Dorset. The additional fact that one of Shadwell's songs used in his *Epsom Wells* (1672) is also sung in this play would tend to confirm his close interest in *Bellamira*.

Does it not often happen that a man who has attained distinction in his art or profession really cares most in his heart for some avocation for the indulgence of which he has had to steal time all his life? One fancies that this may have been true of the dramatist Thomas Shadwell in respect to his devotion to music. Not that he practised it as a secret pleasure. His pride in his powers as a composer and performer was so notorious that no trait of his character gave his literary enemies such an easy target for their satire. D'Urfey makes it part of his ridicule when he caricatures Shadwell in the title rôle of the lute-playing Sir Barnaby Whigg. In Act III he requires Sir Barnaby to sing, to his own confounding, a song the first stanza of which ends with the line

Though I fall a damn'd Poet, I'le mount a Musician.

*The Laurel*, a poem in praise of Dryden, who was in the other camp at that time (1685), consigns *Sh——ll* and his lute to the company of other ragged monsters in the booths at Smithfield Fair. Tom Brown pursued the old poet into Limbo that he might take there one final shot at his vanity. He reports that he "still keeps up his musical talent in these gloomy territories" and is to be seen "thrumming upon an old broken theorbo" (*Letters from the Dead to the Living* in *Works*, 1760, II, 139).

Of Shadwell's skill as a lutenist we have no reliable means of judging. His "thick squab-hand and short thumb-like fingers" may have been able to run a division more nimbly than his satirists allowed. With regard to his compositions we can fortunately decide just how much malice there was in these attacks on his musicianship since several of his songs have survived. Mr. D. M. Walmsley noted in *R.E.S.* 1925, I, 350 two songs by Shadwell which he had discovered in B.M. Add. MS. 19,759, ff. 17 and 20, a collection of music which once belonged to Charles Campelman. The songs are untitled, but the first lines read, respectively: "Fools for themselves will treasure prize" and "Bright was the morning cool the air." In each instance the melody is ascribed to Shadwell. Father Summers has reproduced the songs in his edition of Shadwell, V, following page 384.

Mr. Walmsley supposed these songs were the only compositions of the dramatist which had survived. The music books supply, as a matter of fact, five others, from which we learn that Shadwell put his skill in composition to practical use in the theater. Three of these five songs were prepared for his own plays; a fourth, the one given here, was made for Sedley's *Bellamira*; the fifth, so far as I know, had no theatrical history.

In Shadwell's *Woman Captain* (1679) Sir Humphrey Scattergood is represented as an agreeable dilettante whose main concern is to run through his fortune as rapidly as possible. He is extremely fond of music and frequently calls for a song to pass the time away. In Act IV he orders sung "Let the daring adventurers be tossed on the main," the setting for which is given in *Choice Ayres and Songs,* 1681, III, 6 with no clue to the identity of the composer. In *Comes Amoris,* 1687, I, 36 it is ascribed to "Mr. *Tho. Shadwell.*" In 1687 his song in *Bellamira* was performed. In 1688 two songs by him were sung in his own *Squire of Alsatia,* one of which is reproduced on p. 52. The notes, below, give bibliographical details concerning the music to both. The last of these five songs "Amintor, did you know the pain your absence does create" can be found in *Comes Amoris,* 1687, I, 15.

Shadwell evidently took pains to see that the music used in his plays should be appropriately scored. For example, he notes in the text that "The Expostulation," sung in the *Squire of Alsatia,* is to have an accompaniment of two flutes and a thoroughbass. He boasts of the care he exercised in his *Psyche* to give the composer words which could be fitted to the music "in which I cannot but have some little knowledge, having been bred, for many years of my Youth, to some performance in it." In this opera he chalked out the way to the composer in all but the Song of Fairies and Devils in the fifth act having, so he says, "design'd which Line I wou'd have sung by One, which by Two, which by Three, which by four Voices, &c., and what manner of Humour I would have in all the Vocal Musick" (Preface).

*Psyche* foreshadows the symphonic type of opera which was to be developed in the next century and ultimately perfected by Wagner. It holds an important position in the history of the form. Its significance accrues as much from Shadwell's libretto, designed according to genuine operatic principles, as from the music of Locke and Draghi.[1]

Of Shadwell's wider musical interests we know or can infer a considerable amount. His plays are a treasure-trove of allusion to popular songs and ballads of the day. None of the dramatists had so large an acquaintance with the leading contemporary composers or did so much to encourage their employment in the theater. In the course of his professional career men of such eminence as Humphrey, Banister, Smith, Staggins, Draghi, Locke, Turner, Grabu, Hart, Eccles and Henry Purcell furnished music for his scenes. He acknowledged and praised their efforts and seems to have been on terms of intimacy with some of them.

In his congratulatory poem addressed to the great Italian master resident in England, Pietro Reggio, on the publication of his book of songs, we learn that Shadwell's first master had been John Jenkins, musician in ordinary to Charles I and his son, the second Charles. During the interregnum he moved from one great house to another in the north teaching in the families of the nobility. By Restoration days his style had become old-fashioned, but Shadwell loved the man and reverenced his memory. One of Reggio's excellencies, to his mind, was the generosity with which he honored the older composer. Shadwell implies also in this poem that Reggio had instructed him in music.

These few songs of Shadwell show a musician who is deficient in melodic sense but a careful workman. His style is correct but stiff. Dryden would have said that like his plays it lacked wit, or as we should say, inventiveness.

The music for the song was published in *Vinculum Societatis,* 1687, I, 29. There is an entirely different setting of the eighteenth century on a single sheet (B.M. G. 312 [165]).

Dangerfield's song "When first I made love to my Cloris" that he "made upon a Spanish Princess" and which he sings in Act III, Scene 1 is printed with the melody in *Wit and Mirth,* 1714, V, 212. In Act IV, Scene 6 Keepwell sings, aptly to the occasion, the last three lines of a song put into the mouth of Clodpate in Act IV, Scene 1 of *Epsom Wells.* There the words are printed as follows:

> Her Lips are two Brimmers of Claret,
> Where first I began to miscarry;
>    Her Breasts of Delight
>    Are two Bottles of White,
> And her Eyes are two Cups of Canary.

---

[1] Professor Dent defines the innovations to be credited to Shadwell in Chap. VI of his *Foundations of English Opera.*

I have not found the setting for this.

One of the tunes (p. 209) in J. Playford's *The Dancing Master*, edition of 1690, is captioned *Bellamira*.

## *The Squire of Alsatia, p. 50*

For a discussion of Shadwell's activities as a composer, see p. 104. Shadwell's music for the song is in *Vinculum Societatis*, 1688, II, 22.

In the same scene in which Betty sings "The Expostulation" delicately, Belfond Junior asks Solfa if he has set "that Ode in Horace." He has—that is Shadwell has—and Truman sings it. The ode is "Integer vitae." It was printed as "set by Mr. Shadwell" in *Vinculum Societatis*, 1688, II, 21. In Act III Belfond Senior, to prove to his brother that he can be merry and roar in the Alsatian manner, orders the musicians to strike up "Hark, how the Duke of Lorrain comes." Songs and ballads on this popular conqueror of the Turks were numerous. The music for Shadwell's contribution to the vogue is not extant though there may be some connection between it and the "Duke of Lorrains March" which appears in Playford's *Dancing Master*, 1665, p. 125.

## *The English Frier, p. 54*

Robert King (d. ?1711) entered the private music in February 1679/80, succeeding John Banister whose place was apparently divided between him and Thomas Farmer (Lafontaine, *The King's Musick*, 342, 347). He remained in the royal establishment through four reigns. In 1689, or possibly earlier, he assumed the additional post of composer in ordinary (*ibid.*, 393). In 1690 the distinction fell to him of composing the music for the annual celebration in honor of St. Cecilia for which Shadwell had provided the ode. Cambridge granted him the Mus.B. in 1696.

Following the precedent of Banister, King undertook to offer public concerts. A warrant for this enterprise was granted him by his Majesty's command on December 25, 1689. This warrant, which is printed in *Musical Antiquary*, II, 59, expresses royal approval of King's ability and allows him the sole government of the proposed concerts. All persons are to forbear "rudely or by force to enter in or abide there during the time of performing ye sd Musick without observing such Rules & paying such prices as shall be by him sett down." An examination of advertisements in contemporary newspapers shows that by February 1691 King had established himself next Bedford Gate in Charles Street, Covent Garden, and was performing on Thursday evenings. From the *London Gazette* of March 26, 1691, one learns that Mr. Franck (who had advertised concerts of his own a year previously) is now associated with him. King must have pursued this profitable business over a long period. Hawkins, quoting from the *London Gazette,* notes his concert, with the younger Banister, in York Buildings on January 10, 1697 (*History,* 1776, V, 6).

King's connections with the theater were, for a time at least, very close. Wood states that in addition to his profession of music teaching, he "playes on the Harpsicon in the Kinges Play-House, and playes on the Violin—in Salisbury Court" (Bodleian MS. Wood D. 19 [4] f. 79). If "Mr. Kings Tune to Ye Spanish Fryar" (B.M. Add. MS. 35,043, f. 41) was written for the original production of that play, it must be the first composition of King's to be heard in the theater. In 1684 he set "Ah! why did e'er my thoughts aspire" for Southerne's *The Disappointment* and one song, "Ah poor Olinda"—Draghi providing the other two—in Tate's *Duke and No Duke.* He gave Crowne two songs, "Ah be kind" and "As I gaz'd unaware" for use in *Sir Courtly Nice* (1685). Their association was resumed in 1689/90 when King composed the song given here.

He seems about this time to have been associated also with Shadwell. His music for Shadwell's song "How long must woman wish in vain" which Brady introduced into *The Rape* (1691/92) appears in *Comes Amoris,* 1689, III. In the same year (1690) in which they cooperated in the St. Cecilia ode King provided Shadwell with a setting for "The fire of love" which is sung in *The Amorous Bigotte.*

For some reason which is not plainly deducible King seems to have written nothing for the theater after 1693. Nor did he reprint any of his earlier theater music in his *Songs for One, Two, and Three Voices* (1690). He was a fastidious man, as the extreme care expended in the printing of his songs suggests. He was also at this time beginning to move in the circle of the fashionable great who attended his concerts. From these two facts it is possible to suppose that he was growing a little ashamed of his connection with the players. His friend Motteux had enhanced his popularity among the gentry by publishing many of his songs in *The Gentleman's Journal,* a periodical which conveyed literary gossip, conversation about the arts and popular science to the wits and ladies. Through Motteux in the issue of his *Journal* for October 1693 we get a momentary glimpse of the composer among his new patrons:

My Friend Mr. *Robert King* being lately at the Right Honourable the Earl of *Exeter's* at *Burleigh,* I resolv'd to give him an Opportunity to exercise his happy Talent in Musical Composition, on the Subject of his Lordship's Birth-day then at hand; so I sent him the following Verses, which, not being now adorn'd with the Notes, will indeed rather display my Weakness, than his Lordship's Praise. . . .

Wiseman calls Airy a "hopping, chirping singing Bird." His epithet fits well the contemporary reputation of the actress Mrs. Charlotte

Butler, who played the rôle and whom Crowne seems to have had in mind when he developed the character. She was one of the six principal actresses in the theater when Cibber began his career in 1690. According to Downes she had first acted, in the Dorset Garden Company, about 1673. When Cibber knew her she had arrived at the climax of her fame. He has this to say of her in the *Apology*:

> Mrs. *Butler*, who had her Christian Name of *Charlotte* given her by King *Charles*, was the Daughter of a decay'd Knight, and had the Honour of that Prince's Recommendation to the Theatre; a provident Restitution, giving to the Stage in kind what he had sometimes taken from it: The Publick at least was oblig'd by it; for she prov'd not only a good Actress, but was allow'd in those Days to sing and dance to great Perfection. In the Dramatick Operas of *Dioclesian* and that of *King Arthur*,[1] she was a capital and admired Performer. In speaking, too, she had a sweet-ton'd Voice, which, with her naturally genteel Air and sensible Pronunciation, render'd her wholly Mistress of the Aimiable in many serious Characters. In Parts of Humour, too, she had a manner of blending her assuasive Softness even with the Gay, the Lively, and the Alluring. . . .
>
> (ed. Lowe, 1889, I, 163-4).

In 1692 Mrs. Butler was induced to go to Dublin as a protest against a refusal to raise her disproportionately small salary. After this time she disappears from the English casts. Aside from her success in the two operas mentioned above, her reputation as a singing actress was made chiefly by her performances in *The City Heiress* and *Sir Anthony Love*. The earliest notice of her appearance in a singing part is in the list of those who sang at Court in Crowne's masque *Calisto* (1675). She and Mrs. Hunt divided the modest responsibility of the parts of "Two African Women, or Blacks" while she and Mary Knight filled the more agreeable rôles of Plenty and Peace.[2] Interpolated songs in Dryden's *Cleomenes*, Powell's *Alphonso* and Southerne's *The Wives Excuse* were intrusted to her.

The music for "I once had virtue, wealth and fame" is printed in *The Banquet of Musick*, 1691, V, 1.

### The Wives Excuse, p. 56

According to *The Poetical Register* (1723, I, 30) Thomas Cheek was "educated at Queen's-College in Cambridge, and was a Person of a great deal of ready Wit, and an excellent Companion." It is

---

[1] She performed Philidel, the chief singing part.

[2] As Plenty she wore, appropriately, a "habbit of gold tabby" and a "petticoate of fflowred silver stuffe." The insignificance of her part as the African woman was compensated for, I am sure, by the "habbit of Black sattin Cutt upon gold tinsell: the longets on the sleeves and Bace of silver tinsell with all petty furniture." Somewhere on it there was room for "24 strings of pearl." (Boswell, *Restoration Court Stage*, 307 and 334.)

asserted (*ibid.,* 31) that he assisted Dr. Garth in writing the *Dispensary.* Translations by him of letters by distinguished foreigners like Voiture and Boileau appear in the fashionable letter-books of the time. He could be prevailed on, apparently, for an incidental song when a friend needed one for a new play. For Mrs. Behn he wrote the "second song before the entry" in Act III of *The Lucky Chance* (1686) which begins "No more Lucinda, ah! expose no more." For Southerne, besides this song, he made the words to "Bright Cynthia's power divinely great" sung by Leveridge in Act II of *Oroonoko* (1695). Leveridge set one of his songs for use in Dennis's *A Plot and No Plot* (1697)—"When Chloe, I your charms survey."

In the *Preface* to his *Phaeton* (1698) Gildon confirms this testimony to Cheek's amiable nature. "The Character of Mr. *Cheek,*" he writes, "is too well known to the Witty, and Conversible Part of the Town to need any *Encomium* from me; I am proud of being reckon'd among his Friends, and equally pleased with, and Vain of his particular Approbation of this Play, and the extraordinary Zeal he had shew'd for its success."

For an account of Henry Purcell's career, see p. 89.

The setting of "Corinna I excuse thy face," as printed here, appeared in *The Banquet of Musick,* 1692, VI, 4. The melody alone is given in *Wit and Mirth,* 1707 and 1709, IV, 193.

With the exception of the Italian song performed in the music meeting in Act I, for which no words are printed, settings, by Purcell, for all the songs of the play have been found. "Ingrateful love" which Lovemore prevails on the music master (Harris) to sing at the meeting appeared in *The Banquet of Musick,* 1692, VI, 2. The melody of "Say cruel Amoret" set, so he claims, and performed (Act IV, Scene 1) by the affected virtuoso Mr. Friendall (Mountfort) is in *Joyful Cuckoldom,* 8. "Hang this whining way of wooing," though it is printed in Act V, was also sung at some point in this scene. The setting is preserved with the two other Purcell songs in *The Banquet of Musick,* 1692, VI, 3. Mrs. Butler was the singer of this last song.

### *The Marriage-Hater Match'd, p. 58*

William Mountfort (?1664-1692) was the paragon of the Restoration stage. No actor of his day was so gifted as a performer or so acceptable in his private life to his companions and to the ladies. Cibber, in describing him in the *Apology,* speaks with vivid recollection of his personal charm, the melting tones of his voice in tragedy, the elegance and wit of his style in comedy. He confesses that Mountfort supplied the model after which he patterned his own acting and attributes to him whatever excellence there may have been in his interpretation of Sparkish and Sir Courtly Nice. Mountfort's pitiful end at the hand of the ruffianly Captain Hill assumes the rank of tragedy when one remembers that it was the fatal splendor of his person and character, so ingratiating to all who knew him, that provoked the jealousy of his assassin. The trial of Lord Mohun, who was implicated in Hill's assault, took place in the House of Lords, and his acquittal by that body constitutes one of the disreputable miscarriages of justice among the state trials.

Mountfort was a playwright in his own behalf. Four plays to which his name is attached are entirely his. Two more contain enough of his work to be included in the collective edition of 1720. He characteristically put his talents in the art at the service of his friends. Settle hastens to thank him for the last scene of *Distressed Innocence* (1690) "which he was so kind to write for me" (*Epistle Dedicatory*). Joseph Harris in the *Preface* to *The Mistake* (1690) elaborately acknowledges the gift from him of a scene and significantly remarks in passing, " 'Twould be Tautology to mention his extraordinary favours, which are already sufficiently known, and need not my suffrage."

As an actor whose singing voice made him doubly useful to the theater, Mountfort equalled, though he had no desire to rival, the mercurial Bowman for whom he set the song here printed. Cibber especially refers to the advantage his predecessor in the part of Sir Courtly had over him because of his fine voice. "For he sung a clear Counter-tenour, and had a melodious, warbling Throat, which could not but set off the last Scene of Sir *Courtly* with an uncommon Happiness;[1] which I, alas! could only struggle thro' with the faint Excuses and real Confidence of a fine Singer under the Imperfection of a feign'd and screaming Trebble . . ." (*Apology*, ed. Lowe, I, 129).

D'Urfey wrote the part of Lyonel in *A Fool's Preferment* (1688) around him, and Purcell who composed the music made full use of his voice by designing for him seven of the eight songs which adorned the production. In Act IV he performed the one song from the Restoration theater which has survived in the repertory of modern singers —the *bravura* "I'll sail upon the dog-star."

In his own plays, e.g. *The Successful Strangers* (1689) and *Greenwich Park* (1691), he usually makes an occasion for the character he assumed to sing at least once.

Enough compositions of Mountfort survive to suggest that like Bowman and Leveridge he often made practical use of his training in musical composition. In *Vinculum Societatis*, 1691, III there is "A New Scotch Song by Mr. Mumford"—"Bonny Jockey now with clasping and kissing." *Comes Amoris*, 1693, IV contains his popular "Rise bonny Kate" set to D'Urfey's words. The Library of Christ

[1] Cibber had in mind the passage in which Sir Courtly with bland conceit sings his own "As I gazed unaware" to Leonora who listens convulsed with laughter at his absurdity.

Church possesses an overture and eight tunes for strings, in manuscript (351-2), which suggest from their form use in the theater.

Bowman, the actor and singer, lived to be the Methuselah of the stage. His career which began about 1673 with his employment as a "boy" in the Duke's Company extended to his death in 1739. According to the *Scot's Magazine* for March of that year he was at his death "the oldest Player, the oldest Singer and the oldest Ringer in England" (p. 141). Davies records (note, p. 45, in *Roscius Anglicanus*, 1789) that Bowman was as careful as a coquette in concealing his age and consistently answered to anyone who inquired just how old he was : "Sir, I am very well." He continued to act until a few months before his death.

His parts, which were prodigious in number, included many that made full use of his magnificent bass-baritone voice. The first instance of the exploitation of his two gifts which I find is his performance of Santlow in the anonymous *Counterfeit Bridegroom* (1677). Notable among his singing parts are : Saunter (*Friendship in Fashion*, 1678) ; Crotchet (*The Virtuous Wife*, 1679) ; Atticus (*Theodosius*, 1680) ; Lord Brainless (*Marriage-Hater Match'd*, 1692) ; Rice ap Shinkin (*Richmond Heiress*, 1693) ; Cardenio (*Don Quixote* I, 1694) —the song being Henry Purcell's magnificent "Let the dreadful engines roar"; de Tonnere (*Intrigues at Versailles*, 1697) in which he sang with his wife, the adopted daughter of Betterton; Vainthroat (*The Pretenders*, 1698).

Bowman could turn off a song himself if one were needed in an emergency for some point in a performance. As Lord Froth in *The Double-Dealer* (1693) he sang one of his own compositions—"Ancient Phillis has young graces." The curious will find it in *Thesaurus Musicus*, 1694, I, next to Henry Purcell's "Cynthia frowns" from the same play.

Cibber passes down an anecdote which is sufficient proof of the favor Bowman enjoyed under the reign of Charles.

"*Bowman,* then a Youth, and fam'd for his Voice, was appointed to sing some Part in a Concert of Musick at the private Lodgings of Mrs. *Gwin*; at which were only present the King, the Duke of *York,* and one or two more who were usually admitted upon those detach'd Parties of Pleasure. When the Performance was ended, the King express'd himself highly pleased, and gave it extraordinary Commendations: Then, Sir, said the Lady, to shew you don't speak like a Courtier, I hope you will make the Performers a handsome Present: The King said he had no Money about him, and ask'd the Duke if he had any? To which the Duke reply'd, I believe, Sir, not above a Guinea or two. Upon which the laughing Lady, turning to the People about her, and making bold with the King's common Expression, cry'd, *Od's Fish! what Company am I got into!*"

(*Apology*, ed. Lowe, II, 211).

Playford printed Mountfort's song in the last book of his *Banquet of Musick* which appeared in the year of the play's production (1692, VI, 6). It was reprinted in the eighteenth century in *Wit and Mirth,* 1714, I, 241.

Eight incidental songs were required in the course of the play. In Act II Lord Brainless [Bowman] treats Lady Pupsey to an Italian air to prove his vocal superiority to her lapdog. What this song was cannot now be determined. In the same scene Berenice [Mrs. Lascelles] sings "How vile are the sordid intrigues of the town." In *Comes Amoris,* 1693, IV, 8 this is given with the information that the words were made and set by D'Urfey. The "dul softly Fool" Solon [Mr. Doggett] next contributes the only song he knows, one about hunting that he learned of Nick Stitch, the cobbler in Shrewsbury. The words of this were made by D'Urfey and are printed in his *Wit and Mirth,* 1707, III, 221.

In Act III, Scene 2 Lord Brainless sings during the tea-drinking the song printed here. Soon after he has sat down and received a bow of appreciation from Lady Pupsey's dog, Berenice calls for music. A song, "Bonny lad, prithee lay thy pipe down," the words of which are printed at the end of the play, is performed in response to her request. The music for it, the work of Thomas Tollet, one of the musicians in ordinary, also appeared in *The Banquet of Musick,* 1692, VI, 8.

In Act IV, Scene 1 Berenice sings a snatch of a tune for Darewell's dance. This is followed by the dialogue between Solon and Berenice, "Damon if I should receive your addresses." This has not been found. Finally in Act V, Scene 3 at the grand masquerade which ends in the pairing off of the six couples, two members of the music sing a song in two parts "As soon as the chaos was turned into form." The composer was Henry Purcell, as the fact of its inclusion in the first edition of *Orpheus Britannicus* proves (1698, I, 228).

### *Cleomenes, p. 60*

For an account of Henry Purcell, see p. 89.

A note on Mrs. Butler, the singer of "No, no poor suffering heart," will be found on p. 109.

The words of the song were printed in *The Compleat Academy of Complements,* 1705, p. 116, Song III.

Purcell's music appeared first in *Comes Amoris,* 1693, IV, 1. There is a single sheet version in *Joyful Cuckoldom* (*c.* 1696, No. 19), "A New Song, in the Play called, The Tragedy of Cleomenes, The Spartan Heroe. Sung by Mrs. Butler," and the melody is given in *Wit and Mirth,* 1707, IV, 237. The song is found in two manuscripts in the British Museum, Add. MS. 35,043, f. 5 and Add. MS. 24,889, ff. 21, 46, 66, 89.

A ballad entitled "The Love-Sick Soldier or, the Valiant Comman-
der conquer'd by the Powerful Charms of Fair *Cynthias* Matchless
Beauty. *To which is Added, his kind Answer"* was sung to the tune.
It may be found in *Osterley Park Ballads,* ed. Fawcett, 1930, p. 116.

A dance followed the singing of the song, and vocal and instrumental music is designated in Act III, Scene 2 when the Court is
assembled before the altar of Apis. None of this music exists so it
cannot be said whether Purcell was the composer.

### *The Double-Dealer, p. 62*

For a sketch of the career of Henry Purcell, see p. 89.

Mrs. Ayliff is a representative of the new type of singer in the
late Restoration theater. Before 1690 the dramatic companies seldom
employed professional singers who were not also, or to speak more
accurately, who were not chiefly competent as actors. Certain of these
whose vocal talents were extraordinary, like Knipp, Mrs. Butler,
Mountfort and Bowman, did double duty by singing incidental songs
in plays in which they did not act. But Mrs. Ayliff, Miss Cross and
the celebrated "boy," Jemmy Bowen, of a later generation, were singers who waited their cue in the wings until the characters in the
scene called for music.

We know that Mrs. Ayliff was the original Miss Prue in *Love for
Love* (1695) when it opened the new theater in Lincoln's Inn Fields,
but her assumption of the rôle was compelled at the last minute when
Mrs. Verbruggen who had been chosen to play Prue demanded too
high a salary and failed to get it. With this exception her name is
always mentioned as a singer of interpolated songs, often in costume
as in the second part of *Don Quixote* (1694) where "dressed like a
milk-maid" she sang Eccles's "Ye nymphs and sylvan gods." In 1690
she is mentioned as the singer of one lyric in the semi-opera *The
Prophetess.* Two songs were entrusted to her in Purcell's *Fairy
Queen* (1692), the first of which she sang as a member of Titania's
fairy band (Act II) and the second in the guise of a Chinese woman
(Act V). In the same year her execution of "Ah me! to many deaths
decreed" in Crowne's *Regulus* evoked from Motteux enthusiastic
praise. "[It] is set by *Mr. Purcell* the *Italian* way; had you heard it
sung by Mrs. *Ayliff* you would have own'd that there is no pleasure
like that which good Notes, when so divinely sung, can create" (*Gentleman's Journal,* August 1692, p. 26).

Mrs. Ayliff's career can be followed for a half dozen years through
*The Richmond Heiress, The Maid's Last Prayer, The Double-Dealer,
Love Triumphant* (1693) ; *The Married Beau, Aureng-Zebe* (re-
vival), *Don Quixote* II, *The Fatal Marriage, Timon* (a revival of
Shadwell's play) (1694) ; *Love for Love, Tyrannick Love* (revival),

*Lover's Luck* (1695). In this year she was also a performer in Congreve's St. Cecilia Ode for which Purcell supplied the music.

In Motteux's *Gentleman's Journal* for May 1693 are found three songs composed by "Mr. J. Franck" and sung by Mrs. Ayliff. Since Franck was at this time associated with Robert King in presenting the concerts in Charles Street, one may assume that Mrs. Ayliff assisted at these fashionable music meetings.

After 1695 her name drops from the record. One is safe in supposing that she sang no more in public since from 1695 on the published vocal music from the theater is likely to mention the names of the singers. Can she be the Mrs. Ayliffe, "a Maiden Lady in Hanover-sq." whose death the *Gentleman's Magazine* reports as having taken place on November 2, 1737? (p. 701).

Purcell's music was printed, as given here, in *Thesaurus Musicus,* 1694, II, 7. In 1698 *Orpheus Britannicus* published the song with a figured bass, I, 70. It is from the first of these editions that we learn Mrs. Ayliff was the singer.

The overture and eight act tunes which Purcell composed for the *Double-Dealer* were printed in the posthumous *A Collection of Ayres, Compos'd for the Theatre* (1697). One other song was used in the play, "Ancient Phillis has young graces," which Lord Froth has made on the "old fool that paints so exorbitantly" and sings without any urging in Act III, Scene 3. Bowman who composed it and was the singer held the monopoly of rôles of this sort which required the actor to impersonate coxcombs with a fondness for displaying their vocal abilities. The song was printed in *Thesaurus Musicus, 1694, II, 9.*

### *Love for Love, p. 66*

John Eccles ( ?1650-1735) exceeds even Henry Purcell in the amount of music he composed for the stage. It is possible to trace his connection with sixty-six productions between 1690 and the time of his retirement. He was the son of the eccentric musician Solomon Eccles who burned his instruments, apparently from religious scruples, and turned Quaker. John Eccles became a musician at Court in 1694 in place of Thomas Tollet, another theater composer. By the end of the century, after the death of Henry Purcell, he was the reigning composer at Court and in the town. His position received official recognition by his appointment in 1700 as Master of the King's Music to succeed the dull but worthy Dr. Nicholas Staggins. Eccles composed little except official odes after 1705 but spent his leisure, which he had certainly earned, in angling along the reaches of the Thames. In spite of the facile character of his music, he hardly deserved the sneer with which Anthony à Wood glances at his popularity in his private notes on the English musicians: "Composes

Ayres, of two parts for Common Musitians—a Hedge composer"
(Bodleian MS. Wood D. 110 [4] f. 46).

As Dryden singled out Henry Purcell, after some obtuseness to
his talents at first, so Congreve seems to have especially preferred
Eccles. He sought his assistance in the production of *Love for Love*
and *The Way of the World* and had from him the music for the
masque of *Semele*. Eccles was one of the four composers who com-
peted for the prize, offered in 1700, for the best setting to Congreve's
*Judgment of Paris* and in 1701 he set his St. Cecilia ode.

It is of course impossible to notice individually here Eccles's theater
songs, but the following list of the productions with which he was
associated is, I hope, as complete as can be made from the evidence of
the plays and song-books. It is longer, by twenty plays, than that given
in the *D.N.B.*

1690: Powell, *Alphonso, King of Naples*; Settle, *Distressed
Innocence*.

1693: Dryden, *Love Triumphant* (with Henry Purcell); D'Urfey,
*Richmond Heiress*.

1694: Settle, *Ambitious Slave*; D'Urfey, *Don Quixote* II (with
Henry Purcell); Crowne, *Married Beau*; Anon., *Rape of Europa*.

1695: Banks, *Cyrus the Great*; Congreve, *Love for Love*; Dilke,
*Lover's Luck*; Hopkins, *Pyrrhus*; Granville, *She Gallants*.

1696: Harris, *City Bride*; Doggett, *Country Wake*; J. Dryden, Jr.,
*Husband his own Cuckold* (with Finger); Motteux, *Love's a Jest*;
Manley, *Royal Mischief*; Anon., *She Ventures and He Wins*.

1697: Dilke, *City Lady* (with Finger); Pix, *Deceiver Deceived*;
Motteux, *Europe's Revels*; Pix, *Innocent Mistress*; D'Urfey, *Intrigues at Versailles*; Ravenscroft, *Italian Husband*; Motteux, *Loves
of Mars and Venus* [i.e. the Masque in *The Anatomist, or the Sham
Doctor*]; Motteux, *The Novelty*; Vanbrugh, *Provok'd Wife*; Fil-
mer, *The Unnatural Brother*.

1698: Dilke, *Pretenders*; Dennis, *Rinaldo and Armida*.

(?) 1699: Crowne, *Justice Busy*.

1700: Pix, *Beau Defeated or, the Lucky Younger Brother*; Southerne, *Fate of Capua*; Congreve, *Way of the World*.

1701: Motteux, *Acis and Galatea* [i.e. the Masque in *The Mad
Lover*].

1703: Charles Boyle, *As You Find It*; Rowe, *Fair Penitent*; Anon.,
*Fickle Shepherdess*; Burnaby, *Love Betray'd*.

1704: Rowe, *The Biter*; Farquhar, *The Stage Coach*.

1706: Granville, *The British Enchanters*; D'Urfey, *Wonders in
the Sun* (the ode sung by Orpheus "made to a pretty, but very difficult Tune of Mr. Eccles"—quarto).

1733: Theobald, *Fatal Secret*.

Revivals for which Eccles composed music: Tuke, *Adventures of Five Hours* (*c.* 1700); Dryden, *Aureng-Zebe* (*c.* 1698); Buckingham, *The Chances* (*c.* 1692); Webster, *Duchess of Malfi*; Shakespeare, *Hamlet, Henry V* (*c.* 1690); Shadwell, *Lancashire Witches* (*c.* 1691), *The Libertine* (*c.* 1695); Shakespeare, *Macbeth* (*c.* 1694); Etherege, *She Would if She Could* (*c.* 1693), *Sir Fopling Flutter* (*c.* 1693); Dryden, *Spanish Friar* (*c.* 1696), *Troilus and Cressida* (*c.* 1695); Porter, *The Villain* (*c.* 1694).

Plays in which Eccles's music is definitely known to have been performed but which are not to be found in the play lists: *The Agreeable Disappointment*; *Match at Bedlam*; *Midnight Mistakes*; *The Morose Reformer*; *Self-Conceit or, the Mother Made a Property*; *Surpris'd Lovers*; *Women Will Have their Wills.*

The words of "A soldier and a sailor" are given in *The Compleat Academy of Complements*, 1705, p. 161, Song LVIII.

The music printed here is taken from Hawkins's *History of Music*, 1776, V, 65, where he states that it is the original playhouse version. The early printings of the song do not have the bass which furnishes much of the piquancy of the music. The melody only is given in *Thesaurus Musicus*, 1695, IV, 27 and *Wit and Mirth*, 1699, p. 227. It was also circulated in two single-sheet versions. One of these with a score for the flute is in the British Museum collection of songs H. 1601 (51). The other, much smaller in size, is contained in G 315 (42).

So lively a tune was certain to be popular with dancers. J. Playford put it into the 9th edition of his *Dancing Master* (1696, Part II, 7), the first to be printed after the play's production. Manuscript versions exist: B.M. Add. MSS. 27,932, f. 3 and 29,371, f. 49; Oxf. Mus. Sch. LXV, 7.50; Christ Church Library 360 (treble voice only).

A delightful broadside ballad, "Buxom *Joan* of *Lymas's* Love to a Jolly Sailer: or, The Maiden's Choice: Being Love for Love again," was made by adding further allegorical details to Sailor Ben's narrative. A copy, printed by P. Brooksby, is preserved among the Osterley Park Ballads now in the British Museum (C. 39. k. 6. [61]). Congreve's authorship of the ballad as given in his play has been called in question because of the existence of this broadside. The supposition is that the dramatist merely pilfered the first three stanzas for the use of Sailor Ben. The evidence for Congreve's claim to the verses which he printed is ably summarized by Mr. John C. Hodges in an article entitled "The Ballad in Congreve's *Love for Love*," *P.M.L.A.*, September 1933, p. 953. His argument rests on two facts: the Brooksby sheet may, as far as the evidence of his place of business is concerned, be dated after the play; Congreve is known to have written the broadside ballad called "Jack Frenchman's Defeat" and may have been the author of others.

Several contemporary ballads appropriated Eccles's tune. "The Lusty Lad of London" is among the Osterley Park Ballads (ed. Fawcett, No. 36). "The Saint turn'd Sinner; or, the Dissenting Parson's Text under the Quaker's Petticoats" is No. 80 of the Bagford Ballads (ed. Ebsworth, I, 30). The *Bibliotheca Lindesiana* catalogue (1890) mentions a third, "A Dean and Prebendary." Mr. Rollins prints another, "The French Satyre," in *The Pepys Ballads*, VII, 53.

A traditional set of gestures were required of the singer of the ballad. These can perhaps be more decently imagined by the reader than described. Some idea of how they should be made can be gathered from a note to "The Country Wake" (*Songs Compleat*, IV, 197): "The Chorus to be Humour'd by the Hands and Elbows, as the Souldier and the Sailor." This song was probably used in Doggett's *The Country Wake* which appeared one year after *Love for Love*. As Hob he repeated in it the enormous success of his Sailor Ben in Congreve's play. Doggett, who had earlier made a name for himself as Solon in *The Marriage-Hater Match'd,* Fondlewife in *The Old Bachelor* and Sir Paul Plyant in *The Double-Dealer,* now grew so intractable as a member of the new company at Lincoln's Inn Fields that at the end of 1696 he deserted them and joined the other group at the Theatre Royal. His later vicissitudes as a manager are related in detail by Cibber in the *Apology.*

The first production of *Love for Love* was further enlivened with two other songs. In Act III, Scene 1 Scandal fetches in one to sing "the first Song in the last New Play"—which proves to be "A nymph and a swain to Apollo once prayed." Eccles also set this. It was printed in 1695 in *Thesaurus Musicus*, IV, 25. Eccles put it into his *A Collection of Songs* [?1705, p. 119] where Mr. Pate is set down as the singer.

Valentine in Act IV calls for the "Song that I like." This we learn is "I tell thee, Charmion, could I time retrieve." Finger was the composer and the song is given in *Thesaurus Musicus,* 1696, V, 11. The singers were Pate and Reading. In a revival of the play April 26, 1704, a song by Bowman, "The Misses Lamentation for want of their Vizard-masks at the Playhouse," was added to the others.

### *Oroonoko, p. 68*

The quarto prints the song as "by an unknown hand." The author was Sir Henry Sheeres, as the edition of 1721 confesses. Sir Henry was an amateur poet, an officer in the Ordnance, a member of the Royal Society and a friend of Pepys who was "mighty, though not . . . too fond of him." Pepys left him a ring in his will.

As a boy Raphael Courteville (d. 1772) sang in the Chapel Royal where his father, also Raphael, was until his death in 1675 one of the "gentlemen." The son became in 1691 the first organist of the recently erected church of St. James in Piccadilly. A Raphael Courteville continued to hold this post, not without sharp criticism of his negligent habits, until 1772. His death took place in June of that year. If this incumbent in the eighteenth century was the second Raphael, he is certainly the patriarch of English musicians.

Courteville's songs begin to appear in the music books of the late 1680's and, though they are numerous, only a few can be connected with theatrical productions. His first association with the stage would seem to be the composition of a song, which was an immense popular success, for a revival of Tate's *Duke and no Duke* in 1692 or 1693. "To convent streams" (*Thesaurus Musicus,* 1693, I) was certainly not written for the first production in 1684 for we know that Draghi and King were the composers who furnished the songs then used. "The Prerogatives of Love" was sung in Wright's *Female Vertuosos* (1693). Collaborating with Morgan, Akeroyde and Henry Purcell in 1695, Courteville contributed a large part of the music required in D'Urfey's *Don Quixote* III. *The Alamode Musician* printed in 1698 his "The charms of bright beauty" which, according to a single sheet engraving (B.M. k. 7. i. 2 [72]), Mrs. Hodgson [i.e. Hudson] sang in "Orensebe." The occasion was, of course, a revival.

Jemmy Bowen who sang this song to Miss Cross, with whom he frequently performed for the pleasure of the audiences of the 1690's, appears for a few years in the dramatic records and then vanishes into manhood and private life. Barclay Squire conjectured that he might be the son of the actor William Bowen (1666-1718) whose impetuous, jealous nature led him to attempt the life of Quin and so lose his own in the brawl which resulted. This is a plausible guess for Chetwood remarks that "Mr. Bowen had several Children by his Wife, and a Boy illegitimate" (*General History of the Stage,* 1749, p. 101). One of these lawful offspring may well have been the boy soprano referred to in *Deliciae Musicae,* 1696, III as the "Young Bowen" who sang "Celia has a thousand charms" in Gould's *Rival Sisters* (1695). William Bowen, it is relevant to add, was himself a singer of sufficient ability since the parts given him in Mountfort's *Successful Strangers* and Ravenscroft's *Canterbury Guests* required incidental singing of the actor.

If young Jemmy was, as Barclay Squire supposed, "the boy" among the singers of the Birthday Ode to Queen Mary of 1692, then that occasion marked his first public appearance. In the revival of Shadwell's *Timon* (*c.* 1694) he is still "the Boy." For the next seven or eight years he was in constant request, singing in 1695 in Gould's *Rival Sisters* and the revived *Libertine* (possibly earlier); in 1696 in *The Spanish Wives, The Cornish Comedy* (a dialogue with Miss Cross) and *Ibrahim* (also with Miss Cross as "an Eunuch Boy and a Virgin") ; in 1698 in *The Deceiver Deceiv'd* (conjectural) ; in 1699 the part of a Bramin in Motteux's *Island Princess*; in 1700 in *Love Makes a Man*. The last notices of him that I can discover are contained in a single-sheet song, "Beneath a gloomy shade," used in Baker's *Humour of the Age* (1701) and in the text of Steele's *Funeral* (1701). A song in Act V was sung by "Jemmie Bowin." He can scarcely have been the "boy" who sang twice in Oldmixon's *Grove* in 1700.

The citizens of Richmond should count young Jemmy among the founders of the modern reputation of their city. Until about 1700 it was famous only as a royal residence. In 1696 a place of recreation called Richmond Wells was opened near a medicinal spring which flowed through the grounds of Cardigan House on the hill. A new Richmond became in the next half-century the resort of fashionable London. Jemmy's trills and shakes were in the first days the chief attraction. At least one of the songs with which he delighted the crowds there has survived: "The gods bestow what they require"— set to music by Mr. Franck and "Sung at the New Wells in Richmond by Mr. James Bowen" (Folger, 1363, I).

In the drama of this period a special form of titillation was derived by putting into the mouths of boy and girl actors words whose meaning they were innocently not supposed to understand. The dialogues of Jemmy and the diminutive Miss Cross satisfied fully on this score. In addition both of them were considered by their audiences most exquisite *virtuosi*. Bowen certainly deserved the praise that was lavished on him. Anthony Aston in his *Brief Supplement to Colley Cibber, Esq; His Lives* has preserved testimony to his skill from a critic who cannot be questioned. "As Mr. *Verbruggen* had Nature for his Directress in Acting, so had a known Singer, *Jemmy Bowen,* the same in Music :—He, when practising a Song set by Mr. Purcell, some of the Music told him to grace and run a Division in such a Place. *O let him alone,* said Mr. *Purcell; he will grace it more naturally than you, or I, can teach him"* (ed. Lowe, supplement to Cibber's *Apology,* 1889, II, 312).

The song was first printed in *Deliciae Musicae,* 1696, IV, 1. Its great popularity demanded frequent reengraving. Single-sheet versions were issued by the well known music engravers J. Walsh and T. Cross. Examples of these may be found in B.M. G. 304 (18) and k. 7. i. 2. (71) respectively. Two other versions, lacking the publishers' names, exist. The differences between them are negligible but sufficient to establish the fact that they are typographically distinct. Copies are preserved in Folger 1363, I.

The other songs used in Act II—Courteville's "Bright Cynthia's power" and Henry Purcell's dialogue "Celemene, pray tell me"—

appear with "A lass there lives" in *Deliciae Musicae*, 1696, IV, 3
and 7. Purcell's contribution, for which D'Urfey made the words, was
apparently also sung in *The Conquest of Granada* II (Squire, "Purcell's Dramatic Music," p. 543). The quarto of *Oroonoko* does not
print the words of D'Urfey's song or indicate its use in the scene.
A MS. in the Royal College of Music (1172, f. 1) contains the string
parts for an overture and act-tunes in "Orinoco" by Mr. Peacable
[i.e. James Paisible]. We can therefore reconstruct the entire music
of the play.

## The Island Princess, p. 73

Motteux's "opera," in spite of the scoffing of the critics, touched the
public taste exactly. In the current rivalry between the two stages it
turned the scales in favor of the "old house." In Gildon's *Comparison between the Two Stages* (1702) Sullen is made to say:

But now comes the great Turn which seem'd to decide the Fates
of *Rome* and *Carthage*: The *old House* have a Bawble offer'd 'em,
made out of *Fletcher's Island Princess*, sometime after alter'd by Mr.
*Tate,* and now erected into an Opera by *Motteux*: The Actors labour
at this like so many Galley Slaves at an Oar, they call in the Fiddle,
the Voice, the Painter, and the Carpenter to help 'em; and what neither
the Poet nor the Player cou'd do, the Mechanick must do for him:
The Town had seen their best at the Drama; and now, I was going
to say, the House look'd like a brisk Highway-man, who consults his
Perruke-maker about the newest Fashion an Hour before his Execution; this new fangled Invention was a melodious Whim—
*Ramb[le]*. How? new fangled Mr. *Sullen*? you forget the *Prophetess, King Arthur,* and the *Fairy Queen*.
*Sull.* I remember 'em; and pray are they not new? nay, if you go
to the utmost of it's Antiquity, it came from no elder a House than
*Davenant's,* and that's new enough of all Conscience: but as I was
saying—the *Opera* now possesses the Stage, and after a hard struggle, at length it prevail'd, and something more than Charges came in
every Night: The Quality, who are always Lovers of good Musick,
flock hither, and by almost a total revolt from the other *House,* give
this new Life, and set it in some eminency above the *New* (pp. 33-5).

For an account of the lively literary skirmish which Motteux's
work stirred up see Sprague, *Beaumont and Fletcher on the Restoration Stage,* 1926, pp. 84-6.

Richard Leveridge (*c.* 1670-1758) could turn his hand to anything in the theater. If an incidental song were needed in a hurry, he
would produce one overnight. He could make an acceptable prologue,
set it to music and sing it with a flourish. His magnificent bass voice,
which he managed with unadorned English artlessness, stayed with
him in extreme old age and delighted three generations in the theater.

He sang first on the stage in D'Urfey's *Don Quixote* III (1696). Henry Purcell wrote especially for his execution, so Hawkins says (*History,* 1776, V, 182), the song "Ye twice ten hundred Deities" in *The Indian Queen.* When the Italian opera was at last acclimatized in England in the first decade of the next century, he regularly appeared in bass rôles in which his native directness of manner contrasted delightfully with the artificial grace of Nicolini and Valentini. Otherwise the parts he performed were, as Hawkins says, such "characters as Pluto, Faustus, Merlin, or in short any part in which a long beard was necessary" (*History,* V, 183). He was a great favorite in the pantomimes until 1751 when he took his last benefit.

In 1722 Leveridge became the proprietor of a coffee house in Tavistock Street in the midst of the fashionable district of Covent Garden. Toward the end of his life a public subscription, at one guinea a head, was opened for his support. He continued to sing at public meetings, particularly, we are puzzled to learn, of those for the benefit of the British Herring Fishery (*European Mag.,* October 1793, pp. 243-4).

Leveridge's theater songs defy enumeration. Only a small proportion of them were composed for original productions so that the task of assigning dates to them is difficult. The following list of those in which his music was performed does not pretend to completeness.

1696: Vanbrugh, *Aesop*; Cibber, *Woman's Wit or, the Lady in Fashion.*

1697: Dennis, *Plot and No Plot.*

1698: Crowne, *Caligula.*

1699: Motteux, *The Island Princess* (with D. Purcell and Clarke); Farquhar, *Love and a Bottle*; D'Urfey, *Massaniello* (with D. Purcell and Akeroyde).

1702: Shakespeare, *Macbeth.*

1704: Motteux, *Britain's Happiness.*

1705: Motteux, *Farewell Folly, or, the Younger the Wiser . . . with the Mountebank*; Mac Swiny, *The Quacks or Love's the Physician.*

1706: Farquhar, *Recruiting Officer.*

1715: Anon., *The Beau Demolished*; Anon., *The Mountebank, or, Country Lass.*

1723: Anon., *Jupiter and Europa.*

Leveridge's prologue was engraved as a single song. The second page is missing in most collections. A complete copy, the one used here, is in N.Y. Pub. Drexel 4874.

The music for *The Island Princess* was done in collaboration by Jeremiah Clarke and Daniel Purcell who had in 1697 produced the music for Settle's *World in the Moon.* Leveridge furnished the prologue and two incidental songs.

Motteux handsomely acknowledges their part in its success in the preface To the Reader: "However, I am not willing to attribute it to my self, but chiefly to the Excellency of the Musical Part. What Mr. Daniel Purcel has set is so fine, that as he seems inspir'd with his Brother's wonderful Genius, it cannot but be equally admir'd. The Notes of the Interlude set by Mr. Clarke have air and humour that crown 'em with Applause: And the Dialogue and Enthusiastic Song, which Mr. Leveridge set, are too particularly lik'd not to engage me to thank him for gracing my words with his Composition, as much as for his celebrated singing; Nor must I omit Mr. Pate's admirable Performance, which, with Mr. Leveridge's, gives life to the whole Entertainment."

Practically all of the elaborate music of the play can be recovered. The Royal College of Music possesses, in a four part arrangement for strings (MS. 1172, Nos. 42, 44, 45) the overture and act music by Clarke. The British Museum has in Add. MS. 15,318 the score, elaborately orchestrated for trumpets, strings, hautboys and drums, of the entire work save for a few omissions. It is in the autograph of Clarke. He did not insert Leveridge's Prologue, Purcell's song "Lovely charmer, dearest creature" (Act III, Scene 3), nor the solemn music, presumably by Purcell, for the Temple Scene in Act V. Fortunately all except this last can be found elsewhere.

Engraved versions of most of the songs are scattered in various collections. For Act II: the duet between two shepherds (Pate and Leveridge)—"Cease, ye rovers, cease to range"—in B.M. G. 307 (33); "All the pleasures, Hymen brings," sung by Mr. Magnus's boy, in B.M. G. 304 (73); Miss Lindsey's song as a shepherdess—"The jolly swains"—in B.M. k. 7. i. 2 (36). These three form the largest part of the Entertainment in which "several shepherds advance and express their joy."

For Act III: a song, by the page—"Lovely charmer, dearest creature"—in B.M. k. 7. i. 2 (34). For Act IV: the dialogue "Hold John, e're you leave me," set by Leveridge, in B.M. H. 1601 (188); "Rouse ye gods of the main," sung by Pate as "another Bramin," in B.M. G. 304 (131). Leveridge's famous "Enthusiastic Song"—"Oh cease, urge no more the god to swell my breast"—in B.M. G. 310 (291).

The musical interlude for Act V, written mostly by Clarke, is preserved in the manuscript score, as noted above. Only three of its songs would appear to have been engraved: " 'Tis sultry weather, pretty maid," a dialogue sung by Leveridge as a town-spark, with Miss Lindsey, in B.M. G. 304 (161); "Oh my poor husband," sung by Pate dressed as a "Lusty Strapping Middle ag'd Widow all in Mourning," in B.M. H. 1601 (341); and Cupid's song, set by Leveridge, "Let soft desires your heart engage" in B.M. k. 7. i. 2 (64).

"The Epilogue in the Island-Princess set by Mr. Clarke Sung by Mrs. Lindsey and the Boy, and exactly engrav'd by Tho Cross" survives in the Halliwell Collection of Broadsides (No. 1953) in Chetham's Library at Manchester. The words do not correspond to the printed epilogue, spoken by Pinkethman (quartos of 1699 and 1701). It may have been introduced at the conclusion of the interlude, in which place it will fit logically.

### *Massaniello, p. 77*

See p. 121 for an account of Leveridge, the composer and singer of "The Fisherman's Song."

Leveridge's song was published in at least three engraved single-sheet versions. The one used here is in Walsh's *A Collection of the Choicest Songs and Dialogues* (B.M. G. 304 [115]). The sheet engraved by T. Cross is smaller but also prints the bass part and a score for the flute (B.M. H. 1994 c. 54). A sheet giving the melody only with a flute score is preserved in B.M. H. 1601 (353). The melody is given in D'Urfey's *Wit and Mirth,* 1700, II, 223. There is a manuscript version in Oxf. Mus. Sch. LXV. 5. 22. Chappell observes (*Old English Popular Music,* II, 113) that D'Urfey's "When Harold was invaded" was sung to Leveridge's tune.

The music for both parts of the play was evidently published. The Term Catalogue for Easter 1699 announces "The Songs in the 1st and 2nd Part of, *Massianello* of *Naples.* The Words by Mr. D'Urfey; most of them set to Musick." The entry is repeated in the Trinity catalogue. Neither this volume nor "The Second collection of new Songs and Ballads; with the Songs and Dialogues in the First and Second Part of *Massianello*" (T. C. Trinity 1699) can be unkennelled. Nevertheless a part of the music for the two plays may still be recovered from various sources.

For Part I the last five lines of the Song of Fate (Act II, Scene 1) beginning "No more, no more his brain possess," set by Daniel Purcell, is preserved at the Library of Congress (M 1518 P M). For Part II the "Song in Two Parts, at the Solemnity of Massainello" (Act II) is in the British Museum (G. 151 [56]). "A Dialogue between a Town-Sharper and his Hostess" (Act II, Scene 2) is in the same collection, No. 185. A song of comfort for St. Genaro— "Weep no more"—in Act III, Scene 2 survives in a collection of songs at the Harvard Library, Mus. 512. 23 F.* Miss Campion's two songs in Act IV, both set by Akeroyde, are numbered 72 and 164 in B.M. G. 151. Daniel Purcell's "Young Philander woo'd me long" (Act V) is in B.M. H. 1601 (534).

## *The Constant Couple. p. 79*

Daniel Purcell (*c.* 1660-1717), youngest son of Thomas Purcell of the King's Music and brother of Henry the composer, is entered among the Children of the Chapel in 1679 (Lafontaine, *The King's Musick,* 339). He must have displayed the family genius in music for in 1688 he was appointed to the important post of organist at Magdalen College, Oxford. Presumably he was prepared to content himself with a donnish anthem-writing existence for the rest of his life though one scrap of gossip of his Oxford days shows that he consorted there with the wits. Sir Richard Steele who was often in his company reports that "he exceled so notably in yt Faculty" that all submitted to him and "allowd him ye Title of Pun-Master General" (Bod. MS. Rawlinson D. 833, f.169).

The death of his brother, whom he seems to have loved unselfishly, brought him permanently to London in 1695. There a very different sort of life began for him. His talent was employed at once by the dramatists, who frequently speak of him in their prefaces with admiration. It was not until 1713, when he became organist at St. Andrew's Holborn, that he had time or inclination for another church position. Like Banister, King, Franck and other popular composers of the day he ventured to offer public concerts (*The Spectator,* March 31, 1712).

The first work Daniel Purcell did for the theater consisted in the completing of two scores begun by Henry: a masque in the last act of the operatic *Indian Queen* and music for Act V of Norton's *Pausanias.* The compositions afterwards undertaken on his own account rival in number those of his brother and of John Eccles, the most prodigious of Restoration theater composers. The following list of the plays for which he provided music is, I hope, as complete as can now be made.

1696: *Amalasont* (possibly by J. Hughes; *vid. Biog. Dram.,* 1782, I, 250); Powell, *Brutus of Alba*; Pix, *Ibrahim*; Cibber, *Love's Last Shift*; Hopkins, *Neglected Virtue or, The Unhappy Conqueror*; Granville, *She Gallants* (Grove); Pix, *Spanish Wives* (with Paisible); Behn, *Younger Brother* (with Morgan).

1697: D'Urfey, *Cinthia and Endimion*; Anon., *Triumphs of Virtue*; Settle, *World in the Moon* (with Jeremiah Clarke).

1698: D'Urfey, *The Campaigners* (Grove); Gildon, *Phaeton or, The Fatal Divorce.*

1699: Farquhar, *Constant Couple*; Dennis, *Iphigenia*; Motteux, *Island Princess* (with Clarke and Leveridge); D'Urfey, *Massaniello* (with Leveridge and Akeroyde); Lacy, *Sauny the Scot* (revival).

1700: Cibber, *Love makes a Man*; Oldmixon, *The Grove*; Dryden, *The Secular Masque* [in *The Pilgrim*]; Burnaby, *Reform'd Wife.*

1701: Lee, *Alexander the Great* (revival); D'Urfey, *The Bath*; Steele, *The Funeral*; Baker, *Humour of the Age*; Mrs. Trotter, *Unhappy Penitent.*

1702: Farquhar, *The Inconstant.*

1703: Gildon, *The Patriot, or the Italian Conspiracy.*

1704: Taverner, *Faithful Bride of Granada*; Cibber, *Careless Husband.*

1705: Steele, *The Tender Husband.*

1707: Farquhar, *Beaux' Stratagem*; Rowe, *Royal Convert.*

In addition Purcell composed music for revivals which cannot be definitely dated. "Mr. D. Purcell's Musick in the Comedy call'd the Northern Lass" gives no clue to the production (B.M. d. 24 [21]). Music for a revival of *Macbeth* exists.

According to the article in the *D.N.B.*, Purcell wrote an "opera" on "Orlando Furioso" for the opening of the new Haymarket Theatre in April 1705. I cannot substantiate this statement.

Robert Wilks (*c.* 1665-1732), who as Sir Harry Wildair sang Damon's song, divided the honors in comedy and tragedy with Cibber during the first quarter of the eighteenth century. The early part of his career is closely bound up with the successes of his friend Farquhar who was largely indebted to him for the initiation of his career as a dramatist. The grace and high spirits of his acting contributed largely to the instant acclaim of Farquhar's talents as a playwright, a fact which the dramatist readily admitted. Of Wilks's creation of the part of Sir Harry, he wrote in the Preface to the play: "Mr. Wilks's performance has set him so far above competition in the part of *Wildair,* that none can pretend to envy the praise due to his merit. That he made the part, will appear from hence, that whenever the stage has the misfortune to lose him, Sir *Harry Wildair* may go to the Jubilee."

The part became one of the four in which Wilks reached his true height, the others being Mosca, Macduff and Prince Hal. The *Tatler* of May 24, 1709, concedes that even the "lowness" of the play's dialogue is quite carried off by his acting: "Mr. Wilks enters into the part with so much skill, that the gallantry, the youth, and gaiety of a young man of a plentiful fortune, is looked upon with as much indulgence on the stage, as in real life, without any of those intermixtures of wit and humour, which usually prepossess in favour of such characters in other plays" (ed. Aitken, 1898, I, 164).

Wilks's singing voice must have been well above the average since the parts he took in his younger years frequently required him to sing several times in the course of the play. This is especially true of the plays written by Farquhar in which he acted. As Captain Plume in *The Recruiting Officer,* for example, he sang three songs; as Archer in *The Beaux' Stratagem,* two.

The words of the song are given in *The Compleat Academy of Complements,* 1705, p. 116, Song II.

The music reproduced here is found in *Mercurius Musicus,* September-December, 1699, p. 182. The song was engraved in single-sheet form twice: for Walsh's collection—"A Song in ye Constant Couple or a Tripp to ye Jubilee Sung by Mr. Freeman & Sett by Mr. Dan: Purcell within ye Compass of ye Flute" (B.M. G. 304 [121]) and by T. Cross with the title "The Serenading Song in the Constant Couple" (B.M. k. 7. i. 2. [40]). Leveridge made a setting issued as "A New Song set by Mr. Leveridge. Sung at ye Theater in Dublin" (N.Y. Pub., Drexel 4287) and "A Song set by Mr. Leveridge and sung at the Theatre" (Folger, 1363, IV).

A MS. version of Purcell's music is preserved in Oxf. Mus. Sch. LXV, 5. 6.

Wilks as Sir Harry was required to sing on four other occasions in the play. In Act I, Scene 1 he "walks singing"; in Act II, Scene 3 he sings "Let her wander &" (which I cannot identify). Eleven speeches after the "Damon" song he and Lurewell sing a brief dialogue. In Act V, having no *double entendre* ready at the moment, he sings another unidentified song, "Behold the goldfinches, tall al de rall."

# INDEX TO SONGS

# GENERAL INDEX